The Rhythm of Family

ALSO BY AMANDA BLAKE SOULE

The Creative Family
Handmade Home

The Rhythm of Family

DISCOVERING A SENSE OF WONDER THROUGH THE SEASONS

Amanda Blake Soule with Stephen Soule

Trumpeter · Boston & London · 2011

TRUMPETER BOOKS
An imprint of
Shambhala Publications, Inc.
Horticultural Hall
300 Massachusetts Avenue
Boston, Massachusetts 02115
trumpeterbooks.com

9 8 7 6 5 4 3 2 1

First edition
Printed in Thailand

⊗ This edition is printed on acid-free paper that meets the
American National Standards Institute z39.48 Standard.
♻ Shambhala Publications makes every effort to print on recycled paper.
For more information please visit www.shambhala.com.
Distributed in the United States by Random House, Inc.,
and in Canada by Random House of Canada Ltd

Designed by Lora Zorian

Library of Congress Cataloging-in-Publication Data
Soule, Amanda Blake.
The rhythm of family: discovering a sense of wonder through
the seasons/Amanda Blake Soule, with Stephen Soule.—1st ed.
p.   cm.
Includes bibliographical references.
ISBN 978-1-59030-777-9 (pbk.: alk. paper)
1. Families—Miscellanea, Handicrafts.
I. Soule, Stephen. II. Title.
GT2420.S67 2011
306.85—dc22
2010040450

For Calvin, Ezra, Adelaide, and Harper ~
May you always find peace and comfort
in the beauty of the world around you.

Those who dwell among the beauties and mysteries
of the earth are never alone or weary of life.

~Rachel Carson

Contents

....

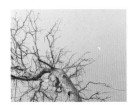

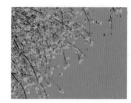

DECEMBER

Introduction

NOTICING

Wonderful things happen in our family when we choose to move slowly through our days. When we stop running and rushing about, we discover more time, energy, and space for the things most important in our lives. By slowing down, our connections with our children and as a family inherently become deeper, our creativity thrives, and we find meaningful ways to fill our time.

The natural world can serve as both inspiration and reward on this journey. For it, too, is ever changing and constantly in motion. As both plants and animals grow, there is an ever present awareness of both birth and death, and the constant passage of time. But this passage of time is a subtle one. One that could be missed if we check in on it infrequently. It is only by spending time in the natural world, by paying attention and noticing, that we see these important changes the earth experiences. This natural rhythm, this subtle changing of the seasons, can act as the heartbeat of our lives. By paying careful attention to the world around us, the slow and even pace can become one that we draw upon in our family lives as well. It can be the rhythm that we all need.

Nature's place as a reward on this journey needs little explanation. For it is there that we—young and old—can and do find much that we need in life: comfort, peace, curiosity, sustenance, adventure, and wonder. In the magical world of the woods, or the shore, or the park around us, our children can truly be free—free to be themselves, free to explore, free to experience the wonder of nature's intricacies around them. In the natural world, we find ourselves much like children—humbled and in awe of what is in front of us. In the natural world, we can connect with our children in a slow, deep, and meaningful way.

Living in the northeastern United States, there is no escaping notice of the changing seasons around us. Each season—and even within that, each month within a season—brings with it such vast differences in our climate and our landscape that it affects our lives in both grand and minute ways. Our day-to-day lives change drastically with each changing season as we shift from snow and ice to mud and rain to heat and sand to harvest and wind. And then shift all over again. These are the rhythms of our environment—the ones we have come to know as our own. With these rhythms in the world around us come the rhythms in our homes, our hearts, our families, and our every day. Our activities change from hibernating from the cold to sowing seeds to exploring the shore, to cutting wood to prepare for the coming-again season of hibernation. Our daily work reflects the changing seasons, as does our play. The snowshoes and ice skates of wintertime give way to mud boots and raincoats, then bathing suits and sandals to cardigans and scarves as our adventures out of doors carry us through the seasons in a year.

I'm enormously grateful for the way the seasons guide our lives such as they do. They provide us with a connection to the earth that I value so deeply as a person—and as a parent wishing the same connection for my children. Noticing the changing seasons connects us to the delicate intricacies and grand miracles of the natural world—birth, life, growth, light, dark, death, and on and on again. And through the noticing of them, we learn not only about the earth on which we live, but we also learn about ourselves and the people around us.

This book was written over the course of a year, through the duration of four seasons. During this year, our son Calvin turned nine, our son Ezra turned seven, our daughter, Adelaide, turned four, and our son Harper turned one. As the pages of the calendar turned, and as we watched the seasons around us change, we documented our time here in these pages. The moments we noticed, the changes we saw, the projects, activities, and dreams we shared in our days together as a family.

Over the course of this year in our family, a new baby was born, someone turned forty, injuries and illnesses happened, much daily work of the home and heart was done, and the play continued—the family adventures were many. And through it all—through the course of a year, through the rhythm of the seasons—we did our best to notice, to celebrate, and to rejoice in the beauty of the natural world that was changing constantly around us. We sought refuge from the stresses of modern daily living in the silence of the wilderness. We found comfort in the gentle waves of the ocean. We were humbled by the awesome seasonal waves of the earth. We grew to really see and know each other even more in the moments of stillness spent out of doors.

"Nature" cannot be defined so easily or singularly. In all of its glorious intricacies, it just is. Exploring, seeking, understanding, and coming to love the natural world keeps us looking at things in forever new and different ways. The sense of play and adventure we receive from our connection to the earth is intimate and meaningful in so many ways. Slowing down allows us to pay attention to the seasons, and paying attention to the seasons helps us to slow down. It helps to ground us in the ever-changing delights of the earth. Losing ourselves for moments at the shore, in the woods, or atop a mountain, we find our center. We feed our souls, and we teach our children. Connecting our children to the earth in this way helps guide them to finding their place in the world—to finding peace within themselves. With the earth as our guide, the seasons lead us on a dance through the year. A year around the sun becomes a spin of the earth on which a whole family rides.

———

My family lives in Maine, deep in the northeastern part of the United States, where our four seasons are extreme and distinct from each other. This book is written from that landscape, though with an eye and a mind on the reality that not all of us experience seasons in the same way. That's the beauty of celebrating the seasons unique to our geography, isn't it? How very different and unique and special they are. Sometimes even varying from year to year. When we embrace an awareness and strive to notice the earth's changes around us—however subtle those might be—we become more aware of something larger than ourselves. Despite our geographical locations, despite our spiritual beliefs about what that might be, it remains true that through the exploration of our natural world, we can be connected in the humility of the earth's splendor.

While I know not all of the seasonal changes we experience and share in these pages will reflect the specifics of your own year and seasons, I hope that they might bring to light some of the subtle or not so subtle variations you do experience in your part of the world. Paying attention to and noticing the ways we are in tune with and connected to the changes in the earth throughout the year can serve as a catalyst for creative play and exploration, family togetherness, and an awareness of earth and self that can only make our lives, our days, our families, and our earth grow stronger with each passing season and with each passing year. May we all seek and find the beautiful places all around us in the years around the sun to come. May we find those beautiful places and get lost in them, wander, daydream, and just be.

Make & Do

A GUIDE TO THE PROJECTS

The projects to make and do in this book were created over the course of a year. They were inspired by the seasons as they occur in our part of the world. However, I urge you to use these projects as they work for your climate and the seasons in which you live, however different they may be than ours. Particularly with the varying climates and landscapes that we all have around the globe, many of the projects will appeal to you and be appropriate for your family at various times of the year.

The projects were all created with family in mind, meaning that each project has an element that involves the work and help of children. Their involvement will vary depending on your child's age, ability, and interest of course, but it's my firm belief and our family philosophy that *there is always a way for everyone to be included.* Look for the ways even the littlest among you can be involved in the process. Keep an open mind and heart as you proceed to seeing things in new ways through the eyes of your children.

The most important thing, I believe, in making projects with children successful for all is to take your time. Move slowly both with your children and with yourself, leaving room for all the exploration and discovery possible.

January

In and Out, Out and In

Like the beating of a drum—in and out, out and in—we follow the push and the pull of where these days take us. Outside, inside, outside, inside. This is the steady rhythm of a midwinter's day. The air is cool, but fresh. Donning scarves and ski boots and layers upon layers of wool, we head out to play in the freshly fallen snow that arrived just the night before in a long, slow, quiet yet strong snowstorm. And so we bundle, all six of us, with all the layers required for this time of year. Some of us—particularly the young among us who are a little more impervious to the cold and full of energy and excitement to see what's changed with this new snowfall—head out faster than the rest. I hear them giggle ahead of us at what they see. We adults linger a little longer with the toddler, wrestling him into the gear he needs to stay warm—and happy—in this weather.

The task of getting everyone dressed and out the door is part of the rhythm of this time of year, and built into our days, just as the clothes rack by the fireplace is built into our furniture for the time being. Hats, mittens, snow pants, scarves, and socks dangle from its wooden frame, and as the snow melts we hear the drip as the water hits the woodstove and the hearth around it. It sizzles and steams, and we are reminded with each drop, that *inside* is warm. For the most part, this is where we are. There is much activity inside these days—so much reading, many games, puzzles, and projects. Crafts and knitting and sewing and wood-working. The projects are endless.

So, too, are the tasks of inside work to keep up with all these little ones—to keep them well fed, clean-clothed, and happy—and their inside creative play. I find most of my time consumed with these daily tasks of home.

Home is our center. Our permanent dwelling that keeps us warm and protects us from the elements of the natural world when those elements are too strong for us to withstand alone.

When outside, I join my little ones on their adventures. I treasure our time spent on skis, snowshoes, ice skates, sleds, and just standing in the snow in our boots with our mouths and eyes open to the bright white sky. There is no end to the humbleness that I feel upon standing in the midst of nature's great work as the snow falls down from the sky. Watching my children take in this wonder—and not only take it in but be a part of it so wholly as they do—is one of my greatest honors as a parent, as a person.

I am in love with the awe and wonder and magic of the out of doors, and equally in love with being inside stoking a fire, baking, and creating a warm retreat for us to return to. In and out, out and in. This is our winter rhythm. This is my family. This is our home. This is our place to come in from the cold.

Snowfall

The flakes drop silently upon his outstretched hand, melting immediately against warm skin, the most genuine of smiles broadening across his face. With curiosity giving way to the purest delight, he giggles and reaches for more. With my child perched comfortably in my arms, this game continues, predictably, and I do not tire of holding or watching him. The snow falls, steadily accumulating. For him, this is another in a long trail of wonders that present themselves in each moment of each day. For me, this is a reminder to view the world as a child and to recall the snowfalls of my own childhood before those memories are buried too deep to retrieve: The days spent with friends in the neighborhoods and forests of a small New England town. Coming home exhausted, cold, and wet, to warm by the woodstove, where my Mom was certain to be ready for me with a hot dinner and fresh clothes. Going back out after dark with my Dad to shovel the day's storm out of the driveway.

Young and strong, my Dad used a wooden scoop push shovel and would run down the hill piling the snow with force across the road. Lying on my back in the fresh banks, staring beyond the streetlight to the stars above, I would replay the events of the day in my mind. With the sounds of my neighborhood drifting to the background I would dream of the future. How would my parents look when they were old? Would I still have my best friends? How old would I be in the year 2000? The sound of my father's voice would eventually beckon my thoughts back to the present. I would make my way to the house, comforted to know that no matter where my life may lead, I could look up into this same night sky and be home again.

The older kids are dressed now and running past into the yard to take their pleasure in the storm of the day. The boys climb high atop the mounds left by the plow and jump off, throwing snow at each other. Adelaide, slowly pushing powder from the railing, examines the shapes it makes as it falls below. Harper watches them, learning. Mama, having patiently attended to the kids and their cumbersome needs of cold weather attire, emerges from the house and we are all together. We laugh and traipse about. The snow is deep and the cold penetrates a bit against our legs as we move across the field, measuring Harper's reaction to his little sled. Amanda remembers to capture the light before it slips away. Her camera clicks with a familiar sound that is comforting to me. The last rays sink beyond the horizon, and we are gathered near the trees, sitting. A streetlight shines across the clouds, and the precipitation has slowed to sporadic, wispy puffs that allow us to look up and catch them

easily on our tongues. Our breath is visible in the dropping temperature of night's air. The lights glow softly from our house and we can see them through the trees, which Adelaide points out.

Before long our hunger reminds us that we must move along and feed the bodies that carry us through the elements, our wintry clothes swishing together as our line transitions toward home. Lulled by the rhythm of his sled, Harper drifts into slumber before we arrive. I imagine, for him, the best of dreams: Dreams of familiar voices and laughter. Dreams of exploration and all the discoveries of which he is capable. I dream for him warmth and love on the coldest of evenings. Scooping him into my arms, we amble up the steps and into that familiar comfort of home in winter. The shift from the icy grip of outdoors into the fire-fueled warmth of home is instantaneous and nostalgic and I remember what it is like to be a child: to be cared for and warm, to feel the love of family without question or doubt.

My son joins me in the yard after dinner as I shovel the walk and clear the driveway. I see him resting quietly in the cold night, and I smile. I remember.

Make

....

Creamy Potato Soup

My favorite winter days are those in which the game of in and out is played all day long. The rhythm beats strongly as our hearts and bellies are warmed by the never-ending pot of soup on the stove. This recipe is a Soule family favorite—sure to please and warm the chilliest of winter wanderers, no matter the age. Make a batch of Everyday Oat Bread (see page 209) for dipping, and you'll have no reason to leave home. Creamy and cheesy and oh-so-warm, this recipe makes us happily snowbound!

WHAT YOU'LL NEED

4 tablespoons butter

3 leeks, halved and sliced thinly

9–10 large potatoes (we like Yukon Gold best of all for this soup), peeled and diced into 1/4" pieces

6 cups cold water

1 cup milk

1 cup cheddar cheese, grated

Sea salt (to taste, approximately 1/2 teaspoon)

White pepper (to taste, approximately 1/4 teaspoon)

WHAT TO DO

Melt butter in a large soup pot. Add the leeks and salt and pepper, and sauté on low heat for 5 minutes. Add potatoes and sauté for a few minutes longer. Stir often.

Add the water (enough to cover the vegetables) and increase the heat to medium. Cover and cook until the potatoes are tender, approximately 45 minutes.

Puree soup. Add milk and cheese. Adjust seasoning to taste. Continue to heat uncovered until just before the soup reaches a boil.

Let the soup cool for a few minutes before serving.

SOULE FAMILY FAVORITE WHOLE FOODS
COOKING BOOKS

The Art of Simple Food by Alice Waters
Feeding the Whole Family by Cynthia Lair
Good to the Grain by Kim Boyce
Nourishing Traditions by Sally Fallon
The Tassajara Bread Book by Edward Espe Brown

Make

....

Wintry Weather Cowls

Growing up and spending most of my life in the coldest of Maine winters, I've learned how important staying warm truly is to being comfortable and enjoying and loving the outside world in the cold winter season. As a Mama now, making sure my kids have the proper gear and layers feels essential for ensuring their love of the outdoors on even the coldest of days. These Wintry Weather Cowls are a perfect way to feel comforted from the cold. (Of course, coming in to a little hot chocolate doesn't hurt either.) These cowls are sized generously enough to fit a large age range from 2 to 12.

KNITTING NOTES

Using a washable wool is ideal for making laundry easy, and a soft wool is ideal for keeping next to little ones' necks. Photographed cowls are knit in Cascade 128 Chunky Solid (100% Peruvian Highland Wool).

KNITTING ABBREVIATIONS

K: Knit
K2tog: Knit two stitches together
P: Purl
Rnd: Round
Sts: Stitches

WHAT YOU'LL NEED

Approximately 100 yds. of bulky yarn, with a gauge of 3.5 sts.
to the inch
One 16" circular needle size US 10, or size needed to obtain
gauge
Yarn or tapestry needle
Stitch marker

WHAT TO DO

Rolled Wintry Weather Cowl

Cast on 57 stitches. Join for working in the round,
and place marker.
Rnds 1–3: Knit.
Rnd 4: Purl.
Rnds 5–12: Knit.

Rnd 13: * K17, K2tog; repeat from * around—54 sts.
Rnds 14–18: Knit.
Rnd 19: *K16, K2tog; repeat from * around—51 sts.
Rnds 20–24: Knit.
Rnd 25: *K15, K2tog; repeat from * around—48 sts.
Rnds 26–35: Knit.
Rnd 36: Bind off loosely.
See below for finishing.

Wavy Wintry Weather Cowl

Cast on 56 stitches. Place marker, and join for working in the round.
Rnd 1: * K2, P2; repeat from * around.
Rnd 2: * K2tog without slipping stitches from left needle, then knit first stitch again. Slip both stitches off needle. P2. Repeat from * around.
Rnds 3–5: * K2, P2; repeat from * around.
Repeat rnds 2–5 for a total of eight times (or to desired length).
Bind off loosely.
See below for finishing.

FINISHING

Cut the yarn, leaving a 12" tail. Thread yarn on a needle, and weave in both loose ends securely. To really show the detail in the cable and get the right fit, be sure to block your cowl.

SOULE FAMILY FAVORITE KNITTING BOOKS

Kids Knitting: Projects for Kids of All Ages by Melanie Falick
Stitch 'n Bitch: The Knitter's Handbook by Debbie Stoller

Da

....

Catch the Sun

Creating sun catchers from frozen ice and the bits of nature found around us is a kids' craft classic. My little ones and I love to make these, gathering everything we can find amidst the snowy ground (or from our seasonal nature shelves). Hanging these ice wreathes and watching them catch the sun and sparkle, and ultimately watching and hearing the drip-drip-drop of them as they melt before our eyes in the glowing sun, is the best kind of slow, marvelously simple entertainment.

CRAFTING NOTE

If there aren't freezing temperatures outside your door, but you'd still like to enjoy the magical, melty sun catcher where you are, there is of course the option of using your freezer.

WHAT YOU'LL NEED

A pie plate, Bundt pan, or tube pan
Bits of nature
Strong string (cooking or gardening twine works well)

WHAT TO DO

1. Begin by gathering your materials. Fill the pan with water 1/3 of the way. Place it outside to freeze.

2. When the water is frozen, bring it inside. Cut a length of string approximately 12" long. Making a loop, lay the string on the ice with the ends near the center and with the loop hanging over the side (this will be the hanger from which you hang the sun catcher).

3. Place nature bits on the layer of ice as you and your little ones desire.

4. Fill the container with water 1/3 more of the way. Let it freeze outside again.

5. When frozen, fill the last 1/3 with water. Let it freeze again. (This multiple layering will help keep all of your nature bits on the inside of the sun catcher, and give you more time to enjoy it.)

6. Remove the sun catcher, and hang it somewhere out doors for all to enjoy! The bits left behind will be a perfect midwinter snack for all the little critters that visit near your home.

Da

....

Grow Your Own Herbs

Growing your own herbs, right in your very own kitchen, makes for a wonderful introduction to gardening. Manageable for even the youngest of children, it's a beautiful way to connect to your food source in any kind of climate or landscape. Not to mention, it's a tasty, fresh addition to your family meals. Kits are available for purchase, but you can do it all yourself with the simplest of tools and materials. The most important advice to remember is to grow what you like and will enjoy eating!

HERBS TO START FROM SEED
Basil
Chives
Lavender
Marjoram
Oregano
Parsley
Rosemary
Sage
Thyme

WHAT YOU'LL NEED

Fluorescent shop lights (if you are in a darker climate)

Containers for potting (anything with a hole in the bottom for drainage; we like to use egg cartons for seed starting)

Seed-starting soil mix

Seeds (see Resources)

A tray for holding the pots (a cookie sheet works well)

WHAT TO DO

1. Choose a location for growing seeds. The kitchen is usually best because it's bright and it's where you will be cooking! But anywhere that has decent daylight and stays approximately 60–70°F during the day will work well.

2. If you are in a dark climate with few sunlight hours, you may want to add fluorescent shop lights to help keep things growing. Lights should hang a few inches above the pots. Depending on how much sun your location gets, you may need up to 12 hours of light time for proper growth.

3. Fill your pots with seed-starting soil mix, leaving approximately 1/2" at the top. Add the seeds, and cover them with soil as instructed on the seed packet label.

4. Place the pots on your tray, then add some water in the tray. When the soil is thoroughly wet (it will be dark), remove the pots and drain any excess water from your tray. Place the pots back on the tray. Mist the plants regularly to keep the soil moist but not so moist that the plants have water sitting atop the soil.

5. Watch your plants grow! Read and follow the seed packet instructions for specifics regarding new growth.

6. Move them up! When the plants start to outgrow their initial containers, replant them in something larger and continue as you've done. Or, if you'd like, move them outside. Wait until there is no more chance of frost in your area, and begin by placing the pots outside during the day. Increase their outside time each day for several days. When the frost danger is past, and the plants have properly transitioned to outside temperatures, plant them in your chosen spot. To do so, find a location that is well drained and gets a good amount of sunlight (6 hours is ideal). Use standard potting soil or compost.

7. Continue to follow the instructions on your seed packet for care as your plants grow. Begin clipping herbs to cook with!

8. Drying your herbs is a wonderful way to keep the fresh, homegrown vibe going all year long. Herbs need to be dried quickly and thoroughly. They can be dried hanging upside down or laying flat on a tray or board. Once the plants are dry, crumble the leaves and place them in airtight jars.

SOULE FAMILY FAVORITE GARDENING BOOKS

The Carrot Seed by Ruth Krauss
The Curious Garden by Peter Brown
Four-Season Harvest by Eliot Coleman
The Garden Primer by Barbara Damrosch
Moosewood Restaurant Kitchen Garden by David Hirsch
Roots, Shoots, Buckets and Boots by Sharon Lovejoy

February

Let Them Play

With excitement, anticipation, and a hurried breath, she rushes in the door, straight to the art cabinet, and begins digging around in earnest. "Ada, what are you doing?" I ask, noticing the steps of mud she's left in her path across the floor. "I'm hurrying!" she replies. "I've got to get a glue stick. I need a LOT of glue sticks. There are some ants, and a really big puddle, and they need to get ACROSS it, and I have to build a boat. A stick boat. It's a big job. A really big job. Sorry, Mama. I've just gotta go." And back out the door she scampers, a pile of glue sticks in her arm, a few more mud prints on the floor.

All of this happens so fast that there isn't time to stop and remind her that she needs to take her boots off before coming in the house. There isn't time to tell her, in my frustration, that I just washed the floors this morning, and that now I have to do it all over again. There isn't time to remind her that glue sticks don't belong outside. There isn't time to have her come back and close the series of three doors that she left open in her wake. There isn't time to worry that her sneakers are on instead of her mud boots.

As I follow her to the door, I'm thinking about all of these things and wondering where to start. What battle do I choose here? What lesson do I want her most to learn—is it one about responsibility, or cleanliness, or taking care of her things? And how is it, exactly, that I am going to fit in washing that floor again before the baby wakes up, before the older boys need me, or before dinner needs to be made. My mind wanders in a circle of "to-dos" and "shoulds." It's a spiral that any parent knows well.

By the time I get to the door I see her already at work. She is bent over with sneakers on (the wrong feet), a fairy dress-up skirt, and a winter's jacket—no mittens, no hat. She has the glue sticks lined up beside her, and she is building a bridge. A bridge across a puddle, just as she said she would. I watch as she lowers her voice to a whisper (surely the ears of those ants must be small ones!) and gently coaxes the ants to cross the stream. "It's okay, little anty-ants! C'mon over!" she says with such love and wonder in her voice. From that beginning, a whole world of imaginary play has begun for her. I know that she will be lost in this play for quite some time. Dreaming, talking to the ants, playing with the mud, and exploring her world—knowing it, loving it, and truly being present in it. I see how the next minutes—perhaps hour—will go. Her brothers might join in. The cat might stop by. She might wander off in search of more sticks and rocks and things upon which to play and build. Fairies might appear. You never do know.

I see all that wondrous play in front of her. I turn to look behind me, and I see the open doors, the mud on the floor, the art cabinet door open, the mud boots sitting dry inside. And suddenly this time—thankfully, this time—I look back to her playing and it becomes clear. I see the fact that I nearly forgot in the details of my day, perhaps the most important thing to remember of all on these busy days of family life: Her work is to play. It is the most important work my little ones can be doing. Time to play, time to be free, time to explore, and time to build bridges for ants crossing the mighty puddle.

But then . . . Oh, then I took it a step further. Not only is this not the time to be having her clean up her muddy shoe prints, but it really isn't the time for me to be doing it either. I have a half an hour—maybe just five minutes, who knows—before the baby wakes up and the next phase of our busy day begins. I will not spend it cleaning my floors. Grabbing a basket of knitting, walking past the mud on the floor (it will be there later, I remind myself), I head back outside again. I find a chair nearby her work, nearby the boys playing catch in the backyard, and I sit. A deep breath of fresh air, closed eyes for a moment to listen to the birds in the trees and the sound of my children happily playing, and I am here and ready in this moment. Ready to play alongside my children.

February Thaw

The thaw came early this year. Days have been spent watching the mercury rise and the rains fall and the snows disappear. We sit in quiet moods as the water gathers in pools and begins its descent to lower ground.

It is far too early to give up on winter and embrace the natural flow between seasons. Yet, just as last spring stretched far into summer with weeks of steady rain, this spring is nudging out winter, mid stride and against rhythm. I worry to myself that these patterns could be the cumulative effect of our years spent using the earth's gifts without repaying our debt back to her. I try to hold back the sadness that creeps in as I look at our children in all their wonder while thinking of how the natural world continues to struggle and fall to the spirit of greed. I strain to imagine my children flourishing in such a place—a place that refuses to revere the sacred. How will I let them know? How can I explain the complexity of this legacy?

I look squarely into the face of a four-year-old girl. Her glimmering eyes and wide toothy smile captivate my heart and inflate it with a willingness to persevere. She climbs into my lap as the water streaks down the windowpane, blowing sideways as it falls. Down.

Eventually, we grow weary of watching the world from inside, like the passing images of a television screen, and we pull on our boots. We slip wool sweaters over our heads and zip our raincoats high and head out into the driving rain of the only home we know. Invigorated from the first step, the storm's energy passes through us and charges our bodies electric and we dash with abandon through the torrent. Nellie dog helps to set the pace by charging across the field in a wild infectious loop that we mimic in a two-legged fervor. The melting frost of midwinter gives way under our feet, and we carry on through the field and down a footpath, toward wherever this rushing stream may lead—a stream that stays hidden save for the heaviest of rains. The children splash and laugh their way downhill without a thought to the swollen river in front of us. Thousands of rivulets converge into one tempestuous cascade of power, and we stare in awe as it makes its way. Down.

We take in the shifting tide of weather that has buried what was here before and left us with today. Through the eyes of my children, I see a world that pulses with delight and possibility. Through the eyes of my children, I see the care they have for this leaf that falls and these seeds that yearn to grow and this river that pushes and falls and forces its way to the sea. We take it in, and I look . . . up.

Somehow, the sun has managed to crack past a thin spot in the clouds. I feel its heat on my face and listen to the sounds of life all around me. Billions of years circling, and here we stand in the warmth of such a star. This piece of rock will survive.

I feel Harper's hands on the back of my head, and I lean into them. He coos to me sweetly, like a bird.

Nellie is sitting calmly at my feet with her nose lifted to the breeze. Eyes half closed.

Calvin has stripped to a tee shirt and is balancing heavy rocks along a downed tree. Strong. Confident.

Ezra leaps from perch to perch and bursts into fragmented song lyrics with unabashed glee. His attire ruffled and unkempt—pants of wool tucked haphazardly into boots of rubber. His style, unmatched.

Adelaide is crouched over a muddy patch of trail, stick in hand, drawing figures against the soft earth. An unconscious stream of conversation, carried with no one or everyone as she works.

I think of Amanda and how happy she will be when I replay this for her later. The kids humming in tune with the vibrations of our surroundings, further proof that we remain deeply connected to this spinning planet, its essence working into our bodies, largely unacknowledged. How much there is to teach. How much there is to learn. How much there is to feel. How grateful I am to witness even one second of its unfolding.

Make

....

A Handkerchief Bag

While there may have been a time in recent years during which hand-kerchiefs were considered old fashioned and unsanitary, I do believe the tide is turning back to these more resourceful, environmentally friendly fabric options. Handkerchiefs are soft, wonderfully multipurpose accesso-ries—to be used as everything from a hair tie to covering a picnic place to, of course, a nose wipe. Once you get in the habit of using handkerchiefs in your family, this handkerchief bag is an accessible and handy way to store them. Our family uses cloth handkerchiefs for a whole host of reasons: because they're beautiful, frugal, because they feel good on your nose, and of course, because they produce less waste on our earth. This handy Hand-kerchief Bag will keep those useful handkerchiefs at your fingertips, free from dust, and ready for use whenever the sniffles arrive.

SEWING NOTES

The seam allowance is 1/2" throughout.

The best fabric for this bag has a bit of weight to it—home décor weight, canvas, and linen are excellent choices.

WHAT YOU'LL NEED

12" zipper
Fabric for the front panels: (2) 8" x 13"
Fabric for the back panels: (2) 8" x 13"
Fabric for the handle: 11" x 4"

WHAT TO DO

1. Working with the handle fabric, fold it in half length-wise and press. Open, and fold each side toward the fold you just created in the center. Press. Fold once again on the center crease. Press. Stitch close to the edge along the opening. (The short ends will be raw edges.)
2. For the front panels, fold each piece in half, wrong sides together, so that they measure 8" x 6½" when folded.

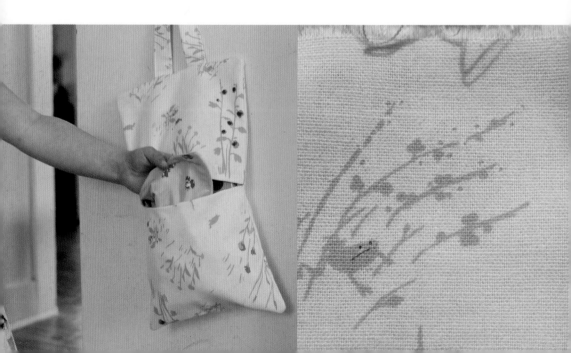

Press. For the back panels, fold each piece in half length-wise, wrong sides together, so that they measure 13" x 4¹/₂" when folded. Press.

3. Place the zipper right side up. Place 1 back panel alongside the zipper's edge, centering it evenly. The folded edge of the panel should lie flush with the zipper's teeth. Pin the zipper in place. Using the appropriate foot and setting for your machine, stitch the fabric to the zipper. Repeat the step for the other back panel.

4. Place the ends of the handle on the right side of the top front panel so the edges are aligned and the loop faces down toward the bag center. Center the handle on the front panel with the ends approximately 1" apart (see photo). Stitch close to the top edge through both layers of the front panel and the handle pieces to hold the handles in place.

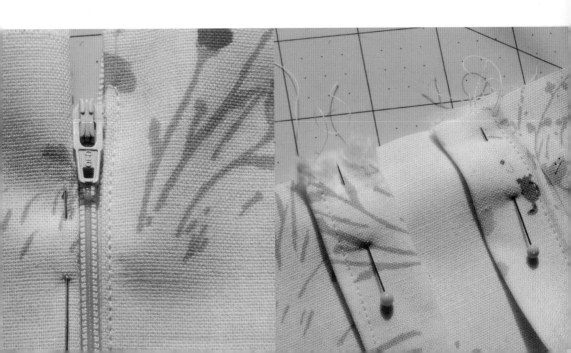

5. Place the front panel pieces on the back panel right sides together. Be sure the front panel pieces are lined up flush next to each other (not overlapping). Stitch around all 4 sides of the bag, reinforcing (by backstitching) at the front opening and handle. Clip all 4 corners, being careful not to cut through your stitches. To prevent fraying, trim all 4 side seams with pinking shears (alternately, you could finish the seams with a zigzag stitch).

6. Turn bag right side out through the front opening. Press. Use a needle and thread to hand stitch the opening, creating a smaller hole through which you will pull the handkerchiefs (sew in about 2" on each side).

7. Use the zipper for inserting a large bundle of handkerchiefs, and pull individual handkerchiefs out individually from the front panel for daily regular use.

Handkerchiefs

Now that you've made a Handkerchief Bag, it's time to fill it with handkerchiefs! You can find the precious vintage hankies at thrift shops, antique malls, or in your grandfather's closet. But making your own can be fun, too. It's a great way to modernize the classic accessory—and individualize them for you and your little ones. Keep them on hand all year long for the allergy, sniffles, and colds that reach your home.

WHAT YOU'LL NEED

Fabric pieces, (2) 12" x 12" (I like to combine a soft quilting cotton or vintage bed sheets and a soft, but somewhat sturdier fabric, such as a lightweight hemp or organic cotton)
Any embellishment desired (such as a freezer paper stencil, embroidery floss, and so on)

WHAT TO DO

1. Prepare fabric pieces according to the measurements above. Embellish the right side of 1 piece of fabric as desired.
2. Place the 2 pieces of fabric right sides together. Pin them in place.
3. Using your sewing machine, and beginning near the middle of 1 side, sew around all 4 sides of the fabric, stopping 3" before your starting point (thereby leaving an opening).
4. Clip the corners, being careful not to cut your stitches.
5. Turn the handkerchief right side out through the opening. Press.
6. Topstitch along all 4 sides of the handkerchief, closing the opening as you go.
7. Use! Store them in a Handkerchief Bag! Keep them handy in your pockets and purses. When it's time for cleaning, wash them by machine in hot water.

Make

....

Sprouts in a Jar

It's always about February or so when I start thinking about sprouting seeds. Surely, it has something to do with trying to eat local and organic. In winter months in Maine, that means mostly relying upon what we've put by the previous harvest season, combined with the root vegetable crops that store well—potatoes, carrots, squash, parsnips, and onions. It means a lot of soup. Delicious and hearty soups, but soup nonetheless! There's nothing like sparking up the winter food months with a little bit of *fresh* green. Sprouts are perfect for this little burst. They give us some nutritious, delicious green but also remind us that spring—and all its green, green growth—will surely return, and everything will once again be alive and growing in the garden. Quite simply—just like the sprouts.

SEEDS TO USE FOR SPROUTS

Alfalfa (perhaps the eas-
iest to begin with—
seen in photographs)
Broccoli
Buckwheat
Fenugreek

Garbanzo
Green peas
Lentils
Mung beans
Sunflowers

WHAT YOU'LL NEED

1 quart glass Mason or Ball jar (wide mouth) with lid (just the rim is needed)

Cheese cloth, cut to a square larger than the jar lid (if your cheesecloth is quite thin, you may want 2 layers to prevent the seeds from falling through)

Seeds (use seeds specifically designated for sprouting)

Elastic

WHAT TO DO

1. Place 2 tablespoons of seed into the glass jar. Add enough warm water to cover the seeds, then add 1" more. Stir to be sure all the seeds are covered. Place the cheesecloth on the top of your jar, and use the elastic to secure it in place. Screw the wide mouth rim on top of the cheesecloth. Soak the seeds for 12 hours in a dark place.

2. Drain the water from the jar through the cloth lid. Add cool water to the jar, and rinse the seeds thoroughly. Again, drain the water. Set the jar in a dark spot to rest at room temperature.

3. Rinse and drain again 12 hours later. Repeat this step every 12 hours for several days or as many times as desired to get the sprouts to a size of your liking (roughly, it will take 3 days for the sprouts to grow 1"–3" in length). Do a taste test to see if they're "done"!

4. Rinse the sprouts in a colander, and dry them on a towel to absorb the water. Place them in an airtight container, allowing the sprouts room to breathe, and store them in the refrigerator for up to a week or so. Rinse the sprouts every few days to avoid a slimy buildup and to extend their life.

5. All seeds sprout differently and taste differently, so experiment with other seeds. Unused seeds can be stored long-term in a tightly covered glass jar in a dark cupboard until they will be used again.

6. Sprouts can be eaten just as is for a snack, placed atop a salad, stacked in sandwiches, or even blended into your Summer Smoothie (see page 141).

Da

....

Heal Yourselves

With the ebb and flow of the seasons comes the ebb and flow of the cold and flu seasons! While the change in seasons may certainly find us with a few sniffles, the earth can also provide us with the tools to heal ourselves. Natural remedies are easy and incredibly fun to make as a family. Some simple Soule family favorites are below, and I've also asked my friend Amy Karol to share a few of her family's favorite healing remedies: the Herbal Vapor Rub and Slippery Elm Throat Lozenges, which have been adapted from the excellent book, *A Kid's Herb Book,* by Lesley Tierra.

Eucalyptus Bath
Such a simple little thing but one that brings us much comfort in times of stuffy headed colds. Simply add three to six drops of eucalyptus essential oil to the running water in your bathtub. Leave out any bubbles or other soap you might normally use. The vapors from the eucalyptus will bring a little relief your way.

Honey Tea
The go-to favorite heal-all drink around our home is our Honey Tea. Simply place a slice of lemon, a slice of ginger (approximately 1/4 to 1/2 teaspoon grated), and a teaspoon of honey in a mug. Pour boiling water over the top. Stir. Remove the lemon if you wish. Drink and enjoy!

Herbal Vapor Rub by Amy Karol
CRAFTING NOTE

Melting solid beeswax to a liquid state is fun and smells delicious, but it can also be a bit messy. I recommend designating a wooden spoon just for beeswax and using a layer of wax paper under your work space. The beeswax, once solidified, can be peeled right off the wax paper and saved for the next time you melt!

WHAT YOU'LL NEED

1/2 cup olive, apricot kernel oil, or your favorite carrier oil
1/4 cup dried mullein, plantain, or lemon balm
1/4 ounce melted beeswax
1 vitamin E gel cap, punctured (squeeze out the oil)
15 drops eucalyptus essential oil
6 drops each rosemary and peppermint oil
4-ounce jar (1/2 cup capacity) or two 2-ounce tins

WHAT TO DO

Heat the herbs over low heat in the carrier oil for 20 minutes. Strain out the herbs, and add the melted beeswax and remaining oils to the carrier oil. Stir. Pour into small jars or tins, and let chill overnight in the refrigerator. The rub will last 1 year or longer at room temperature. To use, rub on the chest at bedtime.

Note: If your child doesn't like the way this feels on her skin, try rubbing a good amount on a cloth and placing it near your child's mouth and nose.

Slippery Elm Throat Lozenges by Amy Karol
Makes about 68 1/2"-round lozenges

WHAT YOU'LL NEED

1/2 cup powdered slippery elm
1/4 cup tea (peppermint, licorice, and/or ginger-lemon
works well)
1–2 tablespoons honey

WHAT TO DO

Make the tea and pour it onto the powdered slippery elm
in a bowl. Stir until a dough forms. Knead until smooth,
adding a bit of extra slippery elm powder to keep it from
sticking to your hands. Pat or roll the dough flat, about
1/8" thick. Using a small circle cutter (such as the cap of
a bottle) cut out the lozenges, re-rolling the scraps as
needed. Smooth any rough edges with your fingers. Let the
pieces dry for a day or two, and store them in a tin or jar.
Suck on a lozenge, allowing it to dissolve and coat your
sore throat.

SOULE FAMILY FAVORITE NATURAL HEALING BOOKS

A Kid's Herb Book by Lesley Tierra
Smart Medicine for a Healthier Child by Janet Zand
Walking the World in Wonder: A Children's Herbal by Ellen Evert Hopman

Da

....

Write a Family Manifesto

It is in the depths of February that I struggle the most with what the seasons provide us. The cold, dark days begin to wear, and it feels as though the bounty and green of spring is still so very far away.

For a few years now, our family has enjoyed the process of coming up with a family manifesto—our family's "declaration of intentions" for the season. It's a wonderful idea to incorporate into any season—those you find challenging and those that feel easy. Stating with intention how you want to live and be in such a specific time of year can only serve to bring us all closer to living the way we would like to be living. Particularly though, in the most challenging times of year, I find this exercise to be a wonderful reminder of the beauty present in even the darkest of days. A reminder to stay focused on that which is most important to me and to us as a family. Work on your family manifesto together, and keep it somewhere prominent in your home for frequent reading and reminding!

Our Winter's Manifesto
1. Follow the sun wherever you find it. Rejoice in the slowly-growing-longer days.
2. Make stuff.
3. With gratitude for the labor of summer and fall, do everything in front of the fire. Morning, noon, and night.

4. Get out there every day, no matter how cold or quick the visit may be. Through crunchy snow underfoot and breath-warmed wool on your face, remember the magic and wonder of it all. Try not to take it for granted.
5. Shake things up, change the scenery, and "get out of Dodge."
6. Wool. Flannel. Capilene. Know them. Love them. Layer them.
7. Gather often with friends. To commiserate. To laugh. To warm the spirit.
8. Savor the memories and bounty of past seasons' harvests. Plan and dream for the one yet to come.

March

The First Day

While the changing of the seasons is a slow and gradual transition, it does seem as though there is always a First Day. The First Day on which the scale tipped and more of our time is spent out of doors than in. The First Day on which jackets are shed. The First Day on which we spy crocuses beginning to appear under the debris that winter left behind. The First Day on which the brave (and usually young) among us walk barefoot upon the earth—feet squishing in gooey, cold, rich mud. "My toes are breathing, Mama!" I hear from my little ones. Indeed, we are breathing.

There's a bursting-through of the doors in these early days of the season. The doors are quite literally opened with extra strength, excitement, and passion—harder, faster, and with more oomph than any other time of year. After such a long winter, with much time spent inside, none of us wants to waste a minute of the sunshine. Each time that door opens, I feel this outward spill of energy as everyone rushes to get as far away from the confines of the house—and sometimes, each other—as we possibly can. Scattering to their respective outside work and play spots, I watch my children take up as much physical space as they possibly can. Just because we can. Because it feels so good to stretch like this. Yes, it feels so much like we are coming out of hibernation.

With the blanket of snow lifting or, rather, melting into the soft ground below, the whole world looks new again. In this time of change, we explore in mud boots and short sleeves. In the mud, in what's left of the snow, in the slush, in the sun. We begin to feel "lighter" out there as we shed those literal layers of winter. Free of layers, outside more and more, we dance in these rays of cool, fresh, spring sun. It is too early for planting, too early for cleaning up from the winter's work, but it is a time marked for rejoicing and celebrating all that is to come. These spring days call to us to bask in the sun while it is shining, with the promise of so much more to come. After the hibernation of winter and before the work of spring, we are in transition on this First Day. We are simply being, dancing in the sun, and greeting the life in front of us.

There is so much to see and reacquaint ourselves with as we greet the raw, brown, bare earth of this in-between season. It is much like re-acquainting ourselves with a long lost friend whose face we have nearly forgotten. Except of course, we could never forget. We feel it in our bones and in our hearts.

On this First Day, the wonder and magic of children discovering amidst the beauty of the world around them is a miraculous thing to watch. The youngest among us is where this miracle is most evident and

literal. I watch as my newly walking toddler begins to navigate his winter-learned skills on the uneven ground of the earth—much different than the smooth, even floors of the inside world we have grown accustomed to. I watch as he lifts one foot and then delicately and cautiously places it back down with hesitation and a look at Mama. Again and again. Stumbling. Taking a few falls, he lands in the mud as a whole other world to discover opens up and distracts him from his previous task of walking. Now, his hands dig in, smear, bury, and smell . . . a little taste, even. Silence in the discovery. Shining rocks with the tiniest newly developing pincher grasp. Exploring. Beginning to know. Giggles emerge from the joy of it. By the end of the First Day, Harper's stumbled steps become smooth, fluid, and knowing walks breaking into a run. The confidence has grown. Knowledge has been gained. And love has grown right there in the muddy steps of a new walker—and in those who once took those steps too. My hope is that in each season of his life there may be a discovery such as this. That there be something that brings quiet discovery and ends in giggling glee. That there be many kinds of sparking First Days in his years to come.

At the Threshold

Eyes closed and smiles wide, we pour from the porch into a new world. A world of welcoming warmth. A world without the all-encompassing cold to which we have all but grown accustomed.

For a family that so loves winter, and all of its many challenges, we have no hesitation to rejoice in its inevitable demise. One by one we step over the threshold and allow the sun to shine on our skin. Its heat is a quilt that generations have gathered beneath to rejoice in its existence, in their own existence.

For a brief, spontaneous second in time, we stand . . . paralyzed.

All of the planning and effort that prepared us for this long season of darkness and cold melts away in one deep and carefree breath. We nurtured our seeds in the spring, helped them to flourish in the summer, and harvested them into the fall to nourish us through these many months of frozen ground and dormant roots. Each stick of firewood removed from its tree to provide a period of comfort while the sun slipped out of a northerner's reach. It all drifts out of us and away on a Saturday morning in March.

The children break free and run, laughing with the rediscovered curiosity that this new light sheds on their everyday arrangements. Free from the confines of their laborious winter garb, they traipse about reveling in the remaining snow. Bicycles are wheeled out, and ridden with unbridled abandon by one, thoughtful whimsy by another, bringing laughter and memories of a long ago season when last they road.

Without thought to how long this stretch of weather might last, we are spellbound. We are entranced by the moment: a symbolic fraction of time that boils away cares and steeps in the magic and wonder of letting go with one steady exhale. Everything that we ever need to know rides through us on a warm breeze and promises that we will remember this. If we are nothing but aware and don't allow ourselves to forget, this sliver of peace and clarity will remain at our side, a gift of realization.

And here we stand. The sound of our children playing, their voices calling us to join them. An eternity of moments leading us to this single, simple one. With all of its perfection. With all of its imperfection. From birth, a lifetime of breathing has led us to this breath.

We are a family. This moment is ours.

Make

....

Tiny Felted Treasure Bowls

There are never enough bowls around for containing all the treasures that my children bring in from out of doors. I created these felted bowls for just that purpose. In such a sweet small size, they will knit up fast and serve as great little gathering spots for all the treasures you and your little ones may find. Felting, the process of turning a knit piece into a felted fiber object, is not an exact science, and the results can vary greatly depending on the temperature of your water, the soap you use, and the wool you've chosen. This pattern will work well with all of those variables and still create a bowl that will be truly one of a kind.

KNITTING NOTES

Bleach inhibits the chemical process of felting, so oftentimes white or light-colored wool yarn does not felt properly. Stick to colors for best results!

You'll notice that as you knit, the fabric will be airy with holes between your stitches. This is good! That space is needed for the felting to happen later. So be sure not to knit too tightly. If you are a tight knitter, you might want to go up a size for needles. There really isn't a wrong way to do this—the fabric will felt no matter what.

The finished size is approximately 3½" in diameter.

See the knitting abbreviations on page 11.

WHAT YOU'LL NEED

1 skein 100% wool, worsted weight (we used Manos Del
Uruguay; 1 skein will make several bowls)
Double pointed needles, size US 10.5
Yarn or tapestry needle
Stitch marker
Mesh lingerie bag
1 tablespoon liquid dishwashing detergent

WHAT TO DO

Cast on 40 stitches. Divide over 3 needles.
Join for working in the round, being careful not to twist the
stitches. Place a marker.
Rnd 1: Purl.
Rnd 2: Knit.
Rnd 3: Purl. (This garter stitch edge will prevent the bowl's
edge from curling.)
Continue in stockinette stitch (knit all rounds) until the piece
measures 3¹/₄" from the cast on edge.

SHAPE THE BOWL

Rnd 1: * K6, K2tog; repeat from * around.
Rnd 2: * K5, K2tog; repeat from * around.
Rnds 3 and 4: Knit.
Rnd 5: * K4, K2tog; repeat from * around.
Rnd 6: * K3, K2tog; repeat from * around.
Rnd 7: * K2, K2tog; repeat from * around.

Rnd 8: * K1, K2tog; repeat from * around.

Break the yarn, leaving a 12" tail. Thread the tail on a needle, draw it through the remaining stitches, and pull tight to close the opening. Weave in the ends.

TO FELT

Place your knit bowl in a mesh lingerie bag and then in the washing machine. Add a pair of jeans to the machine to increase agitation. Add 1 tablespoon of liquid dishwashing detergent. Set your machine to hot wash, regular load. Once your machine is full of water and agitation has begun, check the bowl every so often to check its size. Remove it when it reaches your desired size. Depending on the temperature of your water, it may take 2 cycles to reach the size you want. Remove your bowl before the machine goes through the rinse cycle.

Rinse the bowl by hand in cool water. Squeeze out the excess water gently by rolling the bowl in a towel.

Using your fingers, shape the bowl. Place it over a small bowl, a tennis ball, or other similarly sized object to maintain its shape while drying. Drying can take up to several days.

Make

....

A Terrarium

Oh, how we long for green in the early days of spring! Terrariums are a wonderfully organic and beautiful way to usher in a little bit of green. Moisture evaporates from the soil and plant leaves, condensing on the walls of the terrarium. This cycle of moisture keeps plants growing without frequent watering or attention. In essence, the terrarium becomes its own little ecosystem, a wonderful microcosm for how the larger garden and globe work—such a great lesson for little ones to see and take part in.

WHAT YOU'LL NEED

Potting soil or peat soil
Small succulent plants
Pebbles or small rocks (or aquarium rocks)
Horticultural charcoal, activated carbon (found at your local nursery)
Spoon, tongs, or toy sand shovel
Spray bottle of water
A glass jar or other empty clear container (a fish tank, soda bottles, and so on)
Sphagnum moss or found dried moss

Trinkets for decoration (stones, shells, rocks, acorns, and so on)
Plants (ferns work beautifully)

WHAT TO DO

1. Be sure to properly wash and dry your jar and lid.
2. Use your spoon or shovel to place a layer of small pebbles in the bottom of the terrarium container to provide a drainage area.
3. Cover the pebbles with a light layer of charcoal or activated carbon to filter the water.
4. Add a layer of moss to keep soil out of the drainage area.
5. Place the soil as desired to create the landscape you want.
6. Then, add plants by making a small hole in the soil bed to implant them. Pack soil tightly around them.
7. Add decorations and moss as desired and as room allows.

8. Spray the leaves well with water. Place the lid on.
9. For the first few days, spray the leaves until the terrarium begins to re-create its own moisture, being certain not to overwater it (there should be no water in the rock bed at the bottom layer). If things get too wet, open the lid to air it out a bit. It will begin to settle into itself as a little eco-system in a few weeks.

Do

Follow the Animals

Observing animal patterns and behavior is a favorite pastime of my children. There is so much to be learned by getting to know the other animals with whom we share this earth; we learn not only about the animals, but also about the earth the animals tread upon and ultimately ourselves in the process of watching. When we are at peace, still, and observing other creatures in their own natural habitat, the interconnected nature of everything becomes apparent and felt in a real and natural way.

Children's innate curiosity about the world makes them wonderful investigators for such a task as tracking. Tracking animals needn't be limited to large animals found in rural areas. While tracking something as large as a moose or a deer is quite fun and exciting, there is equal adventure and excitement in tracking whatever may be at your doorstep, wherever you live. Squirrels, skunks, rabbits—whatever the case may be. There are some wonderful resources your family can discover about tracking animals, but here are some very basic things we try to keep in mind about tracking as a family.

1. Tracking is about awareness more than anything. When you begin a tracking journey, do not immediately try to identify what the animal is. Just begin by being aware of the track. Notice all the little details. Inspect it to see if you can discover how the animal landed.

Did it push off or pull away with its step? Do pieces of the track crumble? Just observe and follow. This is the way to truly know the tracks that an animal left behind and eventually to discover just whose steps you may be seeing.

2. Do not hurry. Tracking is not something that should be done in a rush or a hurry of any kind. Allow yourselves the time to wander and be in the wild. Feel the world around you, and take it all in. Tracking is about observation and stillness most of all. Move slowly, quietly, and with great care. This is your best approach for finding tracks and maybe even the animals themselves!

3. Follow the tracks. Once you have properly wandered and stumbled across something you'd like to investigate, follow it! Study it! Measure, draw, photograph, and ultimately identify. A good field guide will be helpful in classifying animal prints for you and make identifying a fun mystery for you and your little ones to solve together.

If this is something of interest to the little ones in your life, and they are given the opportunity and freedom to explore, it will be no time at all before they begin discovering the beautiful, mysterious, and secret world of the animals.

SOULE FAMILY FAVORITE TRACKING BOOKS

Animal Tracks (Peterson Field Guide) by Olaus J. Murie and Mark Elbroch

The Science and Art of Tracking by Tom Brown Jr.

Stokes Guide to Animal Tracking and Behavior by Donald and Lillian Stokes

Tracking and the Art of Seeing: How to Read Animal Tracks and Sign by Paul Rezendes

Da

....

Ask Why

Before my children were born, I remember fantasizing about how we would learn together. How each little bug and insect crawling on the ground that we discovered would send us gleefully skipping inside for the appropriate resource book for the job and happily tracking down our source until we properly identified the creature! Surely, there are many moments just like that—moments when my little ones run inside on their own for the answers they are looking for and, quite often, find. Of course, there are also other times when a wonderful, important question is asked at a less than opportune moment, such as in the middle of making dinner at the end of a long day with four children when someone runs in and asks, "How do you make salt?" or "Do fish drink water?" We want to find the answer, but sometimes it just isn't possible in that moment.

From this need, the I Wonder Why board was born in our house. It's a simple little corkboard on a kitchen wall where questions can go. They're questions that are thought up with an answer hoped for some time in the future. Sometimes, answers are posted later that day. Other times, they're saved up for a cold winter's day when we're looking for a little inspiration.

The ironic and important thing about the I Wonder Why board is that the questions aren't always answered. Interest fades or sometimes the answers become unimportant to the little one who originally asked the question. The important thing, I do believe, about the I Wonder Why board is that questions are being asked. That it encourages questioning, thought, and sometimes discovery of the answers.

BUTTON PUSHPINS

To make these fun tacks for your board, simply use hot glue (or industrial-strength glue) to adhere a flat button (without a shank) to the top of a pushpin that has enough of a head to support the button. Hold the button in place on the tack until the glue dries.

Note: Pushpins and buttons could pose a choking hazard to small children. Please use caution.

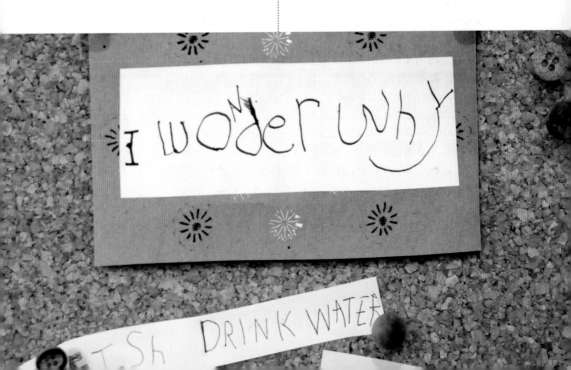

April

The Birds Return

Though they are present year-round, it is in the spring season that we see so many of our bird friends return. The robins appear first—they are the ultimate harbinger of spring's return around here. With them is the proof that the long winter is in its last days and spring is finally upon us. In between the last falls of snow outside our door, it is usually one of the children who spots them first. There is much excitement as the announcement is made, and the whole family rushes to gather around the windows and doors to catch a glimpse. We marvel and stare in excitement at what these small little creatures bring. Many birds follow—the chickadees, cardinals, sparrows, and wrens. We spy the larger ones from afar—the gulls and the hawks. These we heartily debate as a family as to their exact species, more because we all love a good bird debate than anything else. Sometimes we'll run for a camera or the bird book. But more often than not, there is just running for each other to share the news, then standing, quietly watching. There are lots of hushed whispers of, "Do you see . . . ?" and "It's a . . . !" and a whole lot of wide eyes.

With these wide eyes open, we all find silence within and amongst ourselves—a silence that is rarely found in this house of six. Silence as we close our eyes and mouths and open our ears and hearts to hear the birds sing their magic bird songs.

Oh, it is magic. It simply is. These little creatures hold so much beauty for us to see.

It's the last week of April, and my daughter is consumed with the goal of becoming "a bird girl." A bird girl would be someone, by her definition, who all the birds talk about and love, and on whose lap the birds visit for a rest. They know her sweet songs and they know she is a safe place for them to be. In her lap they tell her stories of all the adventures they have and all the things they see in their travels.

This is the story she tells and this is the dream she has as she climbs up into the crab apple tree again this morning. It's her third day doing so, spending most of her days up there in that tree. Her patience astounds me, as she sits on that branch hour after hour. She comes down only when absolutely necessary, and prefers that her meals be brought there. I oblige, because how could I not? She has a dream.

She sings to them, these birds that hover in the top branches of her tree. She coos to them in the softest, sweetest, four-year-old voice, calling them down, reassuring them that she's safe. "C'mon, little birdies, I will love you!" I hear her say as my heart melts.

What she wants with all of her might is to hold one of these birds.

She says she'll let them go—she knows that's the right thing to do. But I hear in her voice the temptation she is resisting to want to catch them. In her heart, I can tell she wants them to be free, but oh, how she would love to hold and squeeze them! A part of her, too, would love to keep them. She plays with the idea of trapping them, how wonderful the cages will be that she makes for them, how happy they will be when they get used to it. This temptation is hard to resist, but she knows. She knows that they cannot be trapped.

I watch this all take place in her days and in her heart, and as I do, I see that the birds carry with them a reminder for me, too. These beautiful flying creatures remind us to appreciate, love, and hold close the small beauty in our hands. We hold it close for a moment, love it and soak it in, and ultimately, let it go. They are not ours; their freedom is their own.

I watch my four-year-old daughter learning this lesson with the birds she loves. At the same time, I'm learning these lessons with her. Over and over throughout her childhood, this will be my role—hold her close, love her, soak her love in, treasure it all so dearly . . . and let her go and grow.

PAPA

Sunrise

Since the day I realized I was going to be a dad for the first time—even before that—I was formulating ideas in my brain about how I would raise my children. Not how we would right all of the injustices perpetrated upon us in our childhood. Not how we'd eat organic or dismiss the TV. Certainly not how, through hard work and discipline, my children would excel and succeed in a hypercompetitive world. Mostly, I would imagine climbing mountains. Outfitting my kids tightly into kayaks for multiday excursions into deep river canyons. Skiing. Before starting a family, these were my passions. My everyday pursuits. I wanted them to feel the connection to the earth that I had felt.

Then, as the children appeared, and multiplied, I realized getting out the door, into the car, and headed toward the beach without forgetting lunch or swimsuits or diapers could be an expedition of which to be proud. And, while introducing my kids to the astonishing beauty and abundant challenges of the natural world is still at the top of my parenting list, engaging in a match of wits and wills with a four-year-old girl and her brothers remains my focus.

Watching them grow and experience life outside the house has been different and undoubtedly more pleasurable than I'd imagined. The thrill of witnessing my children enter the water, its energy running through them as it envelopes their smiling bodies . . . Never had I thoughtfully contemplated how my children's connection to the natural world would be personal, entirely their own, and different from mine. Yet sometimes these paths of connectivity intersect and an experience is shared. When this happens, I recognize their look as my own, and as our eyes meet, I see that they are seeing and feeling the same as I. We are joined through experience, wordlessly sharing time.

Before becoming a parent, I dreamed of the day when my kids could hold their own on adult adventures and keep up at a grown-up's pace. I see now that, more than the shared work of an adventure, their revelation is my reward: Their looks of wonder at each new discovery. Their joy of overcoming their fears. Their determination to remove the training wheels and pedal with arms wobbling, legs pumping, and eyes focused; to fall and pick themselves up from the ground; to break free of that comforting embrace and get back on the bike . . . again and again.

Eventually, their size and skill will allow them into a greater dimension of exploration. In the near future, they will be outdistancing me on our journeys. For now, I am happy to be at their pace, allowed into the realm of the truly magical—a wild and untamed place where imagination remains the greatest frontier. Where the energy of the rivers and the sea blow all around. Where the wisdom of the mountains passes through us on the breeze. Where the lessons of the earth are taught to us through osmosis and immersion into the elements. Where daydreams are encyclopedias and laughter a thesis on self-exploration.

The spirit of my own children reminds me to keep alive that spark of inquisitive learning and constant probing into the unknown. To keep diving for answers, stay suspended, and float in thought. These are not the miracles I had envisioned as a younger man imagining what family life would hold. These are gifts, delivered with sparkling eyes and tiny hands. This . . . this is a sunrise.

Make

....

A Field Bag

Every little adventurer needs his or her own Field Bag. Something to lug all the wilderness exploration supplies in, and something to carry home all the treasures. This sturdy bag can easily be carried over the shoulder, and by adjusting the length of the bag strap, you can customize it to the age of your explorer—whether she be 2 or 52!

SEWING NOTES

The seam allowance is 1/2" throughout except as noted.

I like using wool for the outer fabric of these bags. It's durable, sturdy, easy to wipe clean, and quick to air-dry. I think it also adds a nice rustic flair, which I know that my little adventurers appreciate. If you use wool or a heavier-weight fabric, you may need to go up a needle size on your machine to a size 14.

Anything will work for the outer flap embellishments—sewn circles, children's artwork printed on fabric, embroidery, and more. Vintage outdoor patches make a special touch!

Regular cotton works great for the lining—you might want to use a light color to be sure it's easy to see everything inside the bag. When using a light-colored wool, as photographed, I use a darker contrasting thread color. But use what you like best!

WHAT YOU'LL NEED

Outer fabric: (1) 12" x 28" (for main bag)
(1) 11$\frac{1}{2}$" x 11$\frac{1}{2}$" (for flap)
Lining fabric: (1) 12" x 28" (for main bag)
(1) 11$\frac{1}{2}$" x 11$\frac{1}{2}$" (for flap)
Cotton webbing: 1$\frac{1}{2}$" wide x desired length*
Any patches and embellishments as desired

* To determine the appropriate length, wrap a tape measure around a child's shoulder, across the chest, with ends meeting at the hip. Add 2" to this measurement. As a general guide, I find that 32" is appropriate for the 4–8 age range. An adult might need closer to 40".

WHAT TO DO

1. Cut all fabrics to the measurements listed above.
2. Begin with the outer flap fabric. On the right side, embellish as desired, leaving 3/4" for seam allowance on all sides. Patches, embroidery, fabric circles, and stamping make great additions to the Field Bag!
3. Place the finished outer flap and the flap lining right sides together. Beginning at the center of the top edge, stitch around all 4 sides, stopping 3" before your starting point at the top, leaving an opening. Trim the corners without clipping stitches. Turn the flap right side out through the 3" opening with a turning tool (or chopstick or pencil). Topstitch along all 4 sides, thereby closing the opening you once had at the top. Set aside the flap.
4. Beginning with the outer fabric, fold the piece in half, right sides together, so that the fold is on the 12" side (bottom

of bag). Stitch both sides. Trim the corners without clipping stitches. Press the seams open. Repeat for the lining.

5. Turn outer bag piece right side out. Place the ends of the strap on the right side of the bag centered on the side seams. Align the ends of the strap with the raw edge of the bag's fabric, with the loop of the strap facing down toward the bottom of the bag (see photo). Be sure strap is not twisted. Stitch it in place securely.

6. Place the bag and strap inside the lining so that the right sides are together. Match up the side seams and pin them in place. Beginning at one center, stitch all the way around the top of the bag, securely stitching through the side seams to secure the straps. Stop stitching 3" before you reach your starting point, leaving an opening.

7. Through the opening, pull the outer fabric and strap. The bag will begin to take shape as you do this. You'll need to push the lining down into the outer fabric, spreading it all out. Press the top edge of the bag. Topstitch close to edge along the entire top, which will close the opening. You'll want to have the strap to the right of your needle to avoid getting it caught under the machine.

8. Decide which side will be the back of your bag, and place the wrong side of the flap fabric near the top edge, so that it will "flap" over the bag's opening and cover the bag front. Overlap the 2 edges by 1/2", and pin it in place (see photo). Use a zigzag stitch to secure the flap to bag along the entire edge.

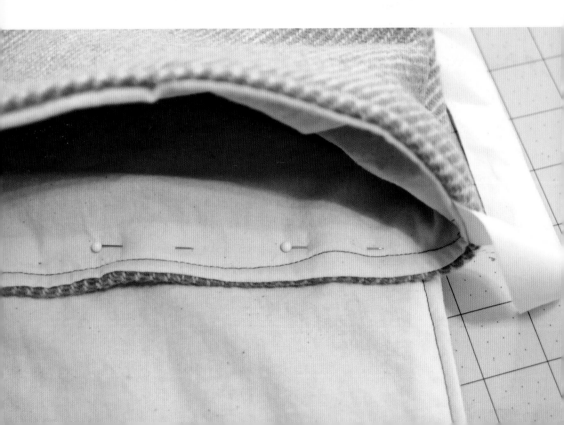

FILL YOUR FIELD BAG!

All one really needs to explore in the wilderness is eyes and ears. But sometimes a few extra little things help make the journey an adventure. You might want to include the following items for your little adventurers.

Binoculars
Bird whistle
Camera
Compass
Insect repellent
Magnifying glass
Nature field guides
Sketchbook and pencils
Small knife or spoon for digging
Swiss army knife (depending on
　age and ability)
Tweezers and jars for collecting
Watercolors

BOOK OF M

MY BOOK OF FLOWERS

Make

....

Nature Notebooks

These simple-to-make notebooks are so handy for all the notes, pictures, drawings, and observations you and your nature lovers might want to record. I keep a fresh stack of these on hand, in easy access for my little ones, for whenever inspiration might strike. It's a wonderful way to use up small bits of leftover paper. Oftentimes in the making of these books, I'll use one of the children's drawings as either the cover or scattered inside amidst the pages for a little surprise. I'm sure you'll come up with endless possibilities for using your notebooks, but to get you started, try the project Our Book of Flowers (see page 104) or Harvest Notes (see page 171).

SEWING NOTES

Your sewing machine is quite handy for sewing paper as well as fabric! Don't be afraid to do so. Paper will, however, dull your needle faster than fabric, so you may want to plan on replacing your needle after you make a few notebooks. You'll also want to use a slightly heavier needle than you would for cotton-weight fabric. I recommend a size 14 when sewing through many layers of paper. Setting your machine to a slow setting will be helpful too.

WHAT YOU'LL NEED

A paper cutting tool (scissors and a ruler are fine, but a paper cutter is especially helpful if you have access to one)
Approximately 10 to 20 sheets of copy paper (for the inside pages)
1 sheet of cardstock or watercolor paper (for the cover)
A bone paper folder is helpful, but not necessary
For flower prints: flowers, hammer, and paper towels, scrap of watercolor paper, glue of your choice (optional)

WHAT TO DO

1. Cut the sheets of copy paper (inside pages) to measure $8^1/2$" x $5^1/2$". Cut the cardstock or watercolor paper (outside cover) to 9" x 6".
2. Working first with the cover paper, use a bone folder (or your hands) to fold a crease down the center of the paper. Open. Repeat this step for the stack of inside pages.
3. Place the folded inside pages into the cover page, aligning the folds along the center.
4. Using a sewing machine, stitch down the center crease. Set your machine to a slow setting if possible, and adjust your stitches to be a little bit longer than you usually would for fabric.
5. Add anything you desire to the front of your book! See the next step for instructions on pressing wildflowers for a decorative touch.
6. Place your gathered flower onto the scrap piece of watercolor paper. Layer 2 paper towels over it and hold them

in place. Using a hammer, make small, even taps across the area where the flower is. This pounding releases the natural dyes inside the flower. When you have covered the area of the flower, remove the paper towel and what is left of the flower. Experiment with different flowers for different effects and colors. Cut your paper to desired size, and glue it to the front of your Nature Book.

Make

....

A Tree Feeder

Creating a Tree Feeder is a simple, fun way for the little woodworkers among you to create their own natural-looking bird feeder. These simple logs blend right in with the natural landscape and make wonderful landing spots for all the flying friends who might be visiting.

WHAT YOU'LL NEED

A fallen branch or log approximately 2" to 3" in diameter
A drill with a spade bit
Garden twine, approximately 1' in length
Bird food (see below)
A branch approximately 2" in diameter

WHAT TO DO

1. Choose a proper branch. Look for something a couple feet in length and native to the area you'll be hanging it in. Think about the natural bends and forks in the wood as a resting spot for the birds, and choose the top and bottom of the feeder accordingly.

2. Drill a hole all the way through the branch, approximately 1" down from the top of the feeder.

3. Using a spade bit, clear a hole in a spot on the log, going only halfway through the log. Repeat this step, making holes in several places along the feeder log.

4. String the garden twine through the top hole and knot the ends to create a hanger.

5. Fill the holes with bird food.

6. Depending on the type of birds you will be feeding, you may want to provide a perch for them to land on. Simply drill a small ¹/₂" hole, approximately 2" below the food hole. Insert a small, similarly-sized stick or twig inside the hole (see photo).

7. Hang the feeder from a spot outside the window and wait for the birds!

A Bird Food Recipe for Your Tree Feeder

Bird food needn't be something that's always purchased—it's incredibly fun to make, especially for the littlest of bird-watchers. You can experiment to find what food attracts birds in your area and what they seem to like most of all. This recipe for the birds in our area is a hit among the juncos, chickadees, wrens, mourning doves, and bluebirds.

WHAT YOU'LL NEED

1 cup peanut butter (the natural stuff—birds don't need
  sugar!)
$1/2$ cup oats
$1/2$ cup cornmeal
$1/2$ cup flour
$1/2$ cup assorted seeds (or purchased birdseed)

WHAT TO DO

Melt the peanut butter in a heatproof bowl. Add cornmeal,
oats, flour, and seeds. Stir well. Form the mixture into
balls with your hands and insert them into the holes in
your Tree Feeder. Store unused portions in a jar at room
temperature, and refill your feeder as necessary.

Da

....

Welcome the Birds

Most children—and many adults, in my experience—have a special affinity for these two-legged tiny creatures that fly. With just a little nest as a place to rest themselves and raise their young, birds spend the rest of their days in the wide world—everywhere and anywhere. For something so small, their home and their travels are so large. In the long cold winter months of New England, in particular, it is much less often that we see the birds. But in the spring—oh, in those precious spring months—the birds return. In those months, their lives become about their babies. Their days are spent building nests, gathering food, and feeding their little ones. Then begins the process of teaching them to fly, and eventually, by summer's end, to be on their own in the great big world they call home.

Preparing for the birds in spring—and assisting them as best we can—is a very special ritual in our yearly rhythm. Marking the beginning of spring, showing us the beauty in small creatures, and sharing with us a broad view of the world, these little birds that we welcome every year bring so very much to our lives.

Make a Bird Basket
So many little bits of what might seem like trash to us are, upon closer inspection, are perfect building tools for the birds in nest building season.

To greet the coming birds of spring, we place a bowl full of such little bits outside where the birds visit. Here, they are able to pick and choose from our offerings for what might help in building a cozy springtime nest. Keep your eyes out and ready for spotting your bits of bird treasures in the nests you see! Some things you could include are leftover yarn, thread, embroidery floss, chicken feathers, scraps of fabric, pieces of hair, raffia, moss, leaves, grass, sheep's wool, animal fur or hair, felt scraps, and more. (Keep your choices limited to nonplastic and biodegradable materials.)

Feed the Birds

It is so delightful to look out one's window and see the interesting and beautiful variety of birds that may visit. And oh, the songs they sing! The beauty of birds is that they appear and live in any landscape and any environment. A city apartment window will attract birds, just as a rural country home will. Different birds for different parts of the world.

Get to know the birds that visit your area, and find out what they like to eat, just as you would in preparing a meal for a new friend visiting your home. Set up feeders around your home—or make the Tree Feeder on page 82—and invite the birds into your yard. It's important to remember that if you begin offering food in winter months to the birds in your area, you must continue to feed them throughout the cold winter season, as they will come to rely upon it. In summer months, it might be best to let them feast upon the seeds and worms found in the natural world.

SOULE FAMILY FAVORITE BIRD BOOKS

The Backyard Bird Feeder's Bible: The A-to-Z Guide to Feeders, Seed Mixes, Projects, and Treats by Sally Roth

Bird Songs: 250 North American Birds in Song by Les Beletsky

Birds, Nests, and Eggs by Mel Boring

Birds of North America: A Guide to Field Identification (Golden Field Guide) by Chandler Robbins

The Boy Who Drew Birds: A Story of James John Audubon by Jacqueline Davies

National Audubon Society Field Guide to Birds (appropriate for your region)

May

In the Ground

I didn't grow up gardening. Naturally, there were people around me who did garden. My grandparents all gardened; I watched them garden, and I enjoyed the fruits of their labor. But it all seemed such a mystery to me—a science I thought I could never understand. But at a certain point in my life, shortly before my own children were born, I decided I wanted a closer connection to the food I ate. I wanted to better understand where my daily nourishment was coming from. So I found a plot in a community garden and just dove in. I had moderate results that year in terms of yield. But the process was an amazingly successful one for me in other ways that I soon fell in love with.

Since that first year, I've never had a season without a garden. Some have been quite grand when time, space, energy, and resources have allowed. Other years—with a brand-new baby at my side, or a smaller apartment yard, or a busy season of change—just a few herbs were planted. A wise farmer friend we know says, "Never let a season go by without planting something." I find that to be so true. No matter how simple or grand the gardening plans are, a wonderful benefit comes from putting something in the ground and watching it grow, year in and year out.

The most revolutionary thing I've learned about gardening in this time is—quite fittingly—the most simple fact of all. *Plants know how to grow.* It is their job to grow. It sounds so simple, really, but the truth is profound. "The nature of this flower is to bloom," Alice Walker, American author and poet, once said. And that simple, beautiful truth is what's precisely so magical about gardening.

Gardening is not something we can control. It isn't something that we can manage. Despite our best efforts, research, and dollars spent on all the latest gadgets or weed management, sometimes a crop just doesn't grow. And to the opposite—no matter what we may do to prevent it, sometimes those plants do grow. Have you ever seen a flower growing through the crack in the concrete? Or seen the roots of a tree literally uprooting the foundation of a house? Their power is mighty; their strength is inspiring. It is nature's job to grow—despite the odds against it, despite the concrete poured over it. Plants will grow.

Once I began to realize that my role as gardener was to nurture the earth, to care for the seeds, and to honor the connection between the two, well, that's when my gardening productivity increased tenfold. And my experience in doing so became even more profound. There is much magic, art, and mystery in the process to balance out all the science and facts and techniques that we can learn. And in this way, a wonderful richness comes from that annual, deep, and nourishing connection to the earth as we work with it to provide the sustenance we need to continue our days.

My time spent gardening is among my favorite moments from the way our days are spent right now. Planting seeds with help from so many little hands. Preparing the soil with the same little ones who sing with glee at each worm unearthed. Checking each morning for the first signs of growth. Spending peaceful moments in the Zen-like act of weeding, often a rare moment of solitude for Mama. Learning with my children just the right time to harvest a vegetable. And ultimately, bringing it all inside and onto our table to feast upon and nourish my family.

Children are the most natural of little gardeners. They have that wonderful balance of carefree confidence that allows them to tromp through a field, pick up earthworms, and fully believe that all they plant will grow, combined with a delicate and gentle nature that reminds them to stop, stroke, and talk with a growing plant as though magic were happening in front of them. Because it is, of course, quite magic.

Put something in the ground. Watch it grow. The nature of this flower is to bloom.

We Live by the Sea

We live by the sea. The level at which all water tumbles and strives to reach. The snows disappear from mountain tops and gather, channeling and converging with other tributaries, in a gravitational pull toward this churning cauldron of ocean. The breadth of its beat and the power of its cycle are a constant metronome to which our days find their rhythm. We sit in its company and revel in its glory. We talk and laugh, run and play along its shores.

Standing at the water's edge, the ocean pulses and sways in waves of energy and potential. The kids watch, staring as if they can see their own possibilities in that horizon, as if its looming depths are their very future—dark and daunting and full of mystery. The more time they spend here and the more they learn from these shores, the less they fear this swelling sea and the farther out they venture, realizing its power is so overwhelming that they need to give in to collaboration rather than conquest. The surf pushes farther in, nipping at their feet. They skitter away into Mama's arms and she lifts them, giggling, safely out of its grasp. Releasing from hugs, she returns them to soft sand and they move back toward the tumult, a little deeper each time.

We spread out along the beach to listen and soak in the surrounding sounds and the rays of a warming sun. We nourish our bodies with food pulled from the sea's salted waters and float boats along its surface with broad smiles and laughter. We challenge ourselves among the great walls of its waves and surrender, bodies crashing in disjointed fury, in praise.

We study it with science and understand its routine but only really feel its pull when we are immersed.

The relationship of my own children to these waters remains a secret. They may move inland on their journey to sit beneath a desert sun, with only the moon to remind them that, somewhere, a tide is turning. They may follow the mountain trail through forests to peaks above the trees where the winds will shout and whisper a tune so familiar. They may move to cities where apartment buildings soar and people push past and taxis swerve in concert with distant vibrations that are felt but not seen. They may never leave its side, captivated by its allure. The boundaries are finite, the possibilities endless.

Its cycle of miracles is shared with us and continues through time. As one life comes to an end, another flutters into being. We carry on and compose new ways to pay homage and rejoice and celebrate in its presence. We frame it through seasons of sun and snow and falling leaves as it balances and levels and shifts under its own weight and invisible lunar forces. On its shores we stand, astounded.

I watch, with my children at my side, and I recall the past. I imagine the future.

I feel the present.

Make

....

Flower Essence Lotion

Making your own lotion can be fun, easy, and safe for children to be involved in. It's a beautiful way to incorporate the flowers, herbs, and plants you have growing around you at various points in the year. This hand lotion recipe is our favorite, but do experiment with the plants available to you in your area. The recipe makes a generous amount, so plan on sharing with friends! (It makes a lovely gift too.)

CRAFTING NOTE

Melting solid beeswax to a liquid state is fun and smells delicious, but it can also be a bit messy. I recommend designating a wooden spoon just for beeswax and using a layer of wax paper under your work space. The beeswax, once solidified, can be peeled right off the wax paper and saved for the next time you melt!

WHAT YOU'LL NEED

A kitchen scale
A double boiler (a heatproof bowl over a saucepan of water will work too)
15 ounces distilled water

A small mesh strainer (tea strainer will work well)

2$^1/_2$ ounces beeswax (available at your local natural foods store, or see Resources for online sources)

6 ounces solid oil (coconut oil, shea butter, and so on)

12 ounces liquid oil (such as olive oil; refined, cold-pressed oils make the best lotions)

Approximately 2 tablespoons fresh herbs/flowers for infusing (lavender, chamomile, rosemary, mint are just some of the herbs and flowers that can be lovely lotion additions)

40 drops essential oil of your choosing, to complement the flower/herb you are using (our favorite combinations: lavender + rosemary, mint + vanilla, chamomile + lime)

A glass, metal, or plastic container for storing lotion

A funnel (helpful for getting lotion into container)

A spatula or wooden spoon

A hand mixer

WHAT TO DO

1. Make an herbal infusion by bruising the leaves of your flower/herb a bit by rubbing them together in your hands or working them with a mortar and pestle. Place the bruised leaves in a mug. Bring the distilled water to a boil, and pour it over the herb. Allow it to steep (yes, just like making tea!) until it reaches room temperature. Strain the herb from the water, retaining the water to use in the next step. Discard the flower/herb.

2. Using the double boiler (or saucepan and heatproof bowl), bring tap water to a gentle simmer. Put the beeswax, solid oil, and liquid oil in the top of the double boiler. Heat the mixture (with the water at a gentle simmer) until everything has melted.

3. Remove the top pan (or bowl) from the heat and water. Set it aside until the mixture reaches room temperature. (If you have a candy thermometer, feel free to use that. But a finger test will be fine too—it needn't be that precise.)

4. Slowly pour the infused water from step 1 into the oil mixture, while beating on high. Beat the mixture until it is combined evenly.

5. Add the drops of essential oil. Mix again.

6. Spoon the lotion out into containers. Label them well, and store the lotion for up to 6 months.

SOULE FAMILY FAVORITE NATURAL BODY CARE BOOKS

Earthly Bodies and Heavenly Hair by Diana Falconi
Organic Body Care Recipes by Stephanie Tourles

Make

....

A Foraged Meal

Foraging in the woods for our sustenance and food is something I have been introduced to in recent years by my very own children as they read and discover and explore such things with people in our community. Before I knew it, sumac, wood nettle, wild leek, and winter mint were making their way into conversation after conversation in our home, and even better—onto our dinner plates! The children love nothing better than going out into our suburban backyard and gathering what they know to create a "backyard salad" for lunch. It's a powerful reminder of the offerings the earth has for us—often ones that we overlook or don't even know about. I asked Langdon Cook, forager and author of *Fat of the Land*, to share his family's favorite foraging food. One that's available in more places than not—the precious dandelion!

Tempura Dandies by Langdon Cook

My kids love tempura—and there's nothing more nutritious than dandelions. Those exasperating taproots pull all sorts of good stuff out of the earth, earning the dandelion the age-old reputation as a cure-all and the Latin name, *Taraxacum officinale*, which translates roughly as "basic remedy." Over the years, I've tried a bunch of tempura recipes for dandelions with wildly varying results. This one is simple yet effective. Whatever you do, make it more watery than you deem appropriate.

COOKING NOTES

Dandelions are plentiful in the late spring and early summer months. When you are gathering, be sure to search in a place that hasn't been sprayed with toxic pesticides. The entire flower and stem are edible, though this recipe calls for the flower heads only. Rinse the dandelions to prepare as you would any vegetable. They freeze quite well, also, so pop a few in the freezer for a taste of foraged summer year-round!

WHAT YOU'LL NEED

3/4 cup flour
1/4 cup cornstarch
1/2 cup ice-cold water, plus extra
1 tablespoon rice wine
1 egg
Vegetable oil for frying
Dandelion flower heads and other assorted sliced vegetables

WHAT TO DO

Pour vegetable oil into a heavy pot or a deep sauté pan to a depth of at least 1" or more. Heat between high and medium high; at this temperature, the tempura-battered vegetables should cook quickly without burning on the outside.

In a bowl, mix the flour and cornstarch. In a second, larger bowl, beat an egg until frothy, then add the ice water and beat some more. Stir in the rice wine. Now add the dry ingredients and mix quickly, not worrying about the lumps. Don't overmix. If the batter oozes off a spoon, it's too thick.

Add more ice water until the batter is watery. (It will seem way too watery for something like Beer-Batter Fish and Chips, but trust me—watery batter is perfect for this recipe.) Now proceed over to the stove with your bowl of batter and a plate of dandelion flower heads. Your vegetable oil should be good and hot by now. Flick in a drop of water to see if it pops and sizzles. Using your hands, dip a dandy in the seemingly too thin gruel. The batter will run off the dandy in sheets but the flower will still be thinly coated and looking rather sad and soggy. Gently drop the dandy into the oil, petals facing down, and *presto!* The flower opens up as if the sun has just come out. (This miracle of kitchen chemistry won't happen if the batter is too thick and heavy.) Cook the dandy on each side until it begins to appear golden. It's really quite amazing to see the dandy regain its form, albeit with a beautifully thin veneer of crispy tempura as its new skin.

Tempura Dandies have an unusual mouth feel. If the batter is right, the outer crust should be crispy, yet being a flower, the overall texture is squishy. I mix the dandies in with other more traditional fare: sweet potato, bell pepper, onion, and zucchini, to name a few.

SOULE FAMILY FAVORITE FORAGING BOOKS

Fat of the Land: Adventures of a 21st Century Forager by Langdon Cook
A Field Guide to Edible Wild Plants by Lee Allen Peterson
The Forager's Harvest: A Guide to Identifying, Harvesting, and Preparing Edible Wild Plants by Samuel Thayer
Newcomb's Wildflower Guide by Lawrence Newcomb

Make

....

Our Book of Flowers

Once you've made a Nature Notebook (see page 79; or found an empty journal or book to use), you might want to document the flowers that you see! Our children each have their very own My Book of Flowers that they make and keep from season to season and year to year to sketch, paint, or note the flowers they've seen. On walks or trips just around our backyard, they may find something special they want to bring inside to draw. They use whatever method inspires them at the moment or whatever we have the time and space for at any given time. Watercolors, charcoal pencils, colored pencils, pastels—the list is endless. Use the instructions on pages 80–81 to create pressed flower art!

Bringing in a flower, the children use guidebooks to identify it if it's one that's new to them. Sometimes notes are added to the page "Dandelion from Grammy's House" or "The First Violet of 2010." Of course, the sky is the limit with the possibilities for your very own Nature Books. What about My Book of Leaves? Or My Book of Rocks? So many possibilities! So much beautiful nature-filled children's art!

SOULE FAMILY FAVORITE FLOWER BOOKS

A Child's Book of Flowers by Janet Marsh
The Flowers' Festival by Elsa Beskow
National Audubon Society Field Guide to Wildflowers

Da

....

Bloom Branches

In the early spring days, what a true treat it can be to bring a little bit of the coming blooms inside to enjoy a bit earlier than we will on the outside. Bringing spring blooming shrub and tree branches into the warmth of our homes is an easy, fun way to bring a little bit of spring magic in the dark days of winter's end, and it helps connect us all to the process of growth.

WHAT TO DO

1. Cut your branches at the top of the plant just when the buds are beginning to swell. Cut at a sharp angle.
2. Place the branches in a bucket of cold water in a cool room (a garage, basement, or off-season porch works well) for a few days, before transitioning them all the way inside.
3. Fill a vase with cool water. Cut the branches one more time, and place them in the water-filled vase.
4. Keep the vase full of water always. Change the water often to keep the stems from rotting.

TREES THAT WORK WELL FOR FORCING BLOOMS

Crab apple and apple (shown in photograph)
Dogwood
Flowering cherry
Forsythia
Lilac
Pussy willow
Quince

June

Home at Sea

There is so much fullness in our days. So much activity, so much flurry, sometimes so much chaos. With four little ones, there's always something going on—usually four things going on—in any given moment. And yet, I find that if I'm open to receiving them, there are so very many moments of peace and quiet and still in the day, too.

Harper's days right now are spent crawling around in circles, taking steps, learning new words, and so many other things going on at once. It's a time of big change for him, and so much growth from day to day. But I watch him as he goes back and forth between these things—sometimes in joy, sometimes in frustration—and stops. He does stop-by's, crawling up to sit with me for a minute. He nestles into my shoulder, he kisses and smiles. He takes a few breaths there in my arms, and then he's off again. It's just a little check-in for him, a reconnection with his center (located, of course, still in the arms of Mama or Papa).

It's so clear with babies, and yet the same happens with my older children in less literal ways. I watch them grow and struggle and thrive with independence and growth—and then retreat "home." It connects us all; it's what allows us to go back out and seek more adventure and challenge and life.

Sometimes to move ahead we must go back to where we came from. To discover and strengthen our current connection to the earth and its seasons, we must sometimes visit with our first connection to it. All of us—to one degree or another—have some childhood connection to the earth. Hiking in the woods with your family, swinging on your front porch swing feeling the wind in your mouth, taking the long way home from school through the park, visiting a grandparents' farm.

We may be just as connected to that original source as we once were. Or we may, with time and adulthood, have lost our way. Sometimes reconnecting with that original relationship is just the thing we need to do to find solace now. Seeking out these special places as adults, and remembering them, is helpful in building our adult relationship with the earth, with our children, and with ourselves.

I grew up on the coast of Maine. Quite literally, on the coast of Maine. The bedroom in which I spent my childhood nights sat a dreamy 200 yards from the coastline. As I fell asleep each night, I could hear the noise of the harbor, the busyness of the ships passing by—and if I was very quiet, and very still, and very lucky, the sound of the waves. These waves lulled me to sleep and comforted me. Today, they continue to do that. The original relationship I had still remains the strongest. As I find myself now in times of challenge, personal struggle, or confusion, I feel a magnetic pull to the ocean, as if I'm being pulled back there—and back to myself—for connection and reflection and comforting peace.

I watch as my children begin to know and rely upon the healing power of the natural world. I see my son run to the woods when tears are welling up in his eyes with the frustration of being a child and growing up. I keep an eye on him from the window and see how he runs to throw himself in the arms of the woods, just as he sometimes does in my own arms. It's a slow transition of being safe within my sight, while seeking comfort outside of our doors. And so begins the transition and growth and independence of a growing child.

Whether we remember feeling this connection to the earth as children or not, it's never too late in our lives to find it—or reclaim it—now. Just like the child in need of the silent and open hug of a mother or the woods, we too need these things. We must keep looking and searching for the places that bring us peace, dreams, and comfort throughout our lives. And when we do find them, share them with the ones we love.

Summer Place

The year was 1976. I was seven years old. The memories I have of those days are awash in a childhood haze of flowery 70s clothes, big belt buckles, long cars, and short shorts. Our neighborhood was crowded with kids that would gather every evening to play kick the can or hide and seek. My older sisters would find a hidden spot to play truth or dare with their friends, a gregarious bunch with long crazy hair and sideburns and big smiles. What was a complex and confusing time for our country could not have been more simple or beautiful for a seven-year-old boy in the safe hold of his family, his land.

When the Maine weather turned hot and humid, we would head north to our small cabin on a cold, spring-fed lake that was less than an hour from our house. This allowed my Dad to commute to work each day and allowed my Mom and the four of us to revel, for a brief time, in the splendor of life in the trees. Life on the water.

I would wake early and sit on the dock, the morning sun just heating up, the lake void of the faintest ripple. "Just like a bottle," my Dad would say. I would check my bait trap that I set the night before and transfer shiners into a bait bucket for safekeeping. Occasionally, I'd have an eel in my trap and I'd let it go on the sand and watch as it instinctually slithered its way back to the water. I'd lie on my belly and scan the lake bottom for signs of life. Most mornings, my Mom would join me and have her coffee and read a book as I woke up with the world. I remember feeling as if I'd lived a lifetime before my sisters and little brother had stirred from their beds. We'd have aunts and uncles and cousins and grandparents come to visit and stay for a few days or a weekend. I was always so excited and proud to show them all of the things there were to do at our summer place: the best places to catch frogs, the best rocks from which to jump into the lake, the trail along the water to my friend's camp. I showed them all of my secret haunts . . . except one.

Even at seven years old, I remember this compelling need to have a space of my own. A spot where I could sit and just be silent. To think my own thoughts without the background noise that a middle child becomes so accustomed to hearing. At home, I could retreat to the basement or the garage where no one else cared to spend much time. But my spot at the lake was different. It was purely magical, and I remember its detail to this day. I would walk there slowly, purposefully alone, and without fanfare. The trees along the bank were a group of hardwoods with some small cedars in between forming a tight walkway that probably went unnoticed by those over four feet tall. I could slip neatly out of sight and onto a perfectly flat rock that sat snuggly against the shore and offered me a hidden retreat that I never divulged in our summers on the lake. The water was absolutely clear and the bottom here, only a couple of feet deep, was covered with the finest sand.

Here. Here I could sit and just listen. As the waves slapped against the rocks, I could hear what the lake was telling me. Its subtle reminder to me that it had been here for a very, very long time. From this minor place I learned to form my own opinions and I understood that my relationship with the earth was unique. It was mine.

From this space, I'd hear my mother call for me and we'd walk the dirt road in the late afternoon sun and pick raspberries and eat them. Dad would meet us on his way home from work, and we'd climb into the bed of his truck for a ride back. After dinner, he and I would gear up and take our little fishing boat out on the lake. We'd use my bait and fish for salmon and lake trout on our way to the spring to fill up the water jugs. He'd let me steer for a while when we were in the deep water. When I was in a boat with my Dad, everything was right. Impending dark would inevitably drive us toward home, and my awaiting bed held the dream that tomorrow could be just like today. The summers went by too fast though, and it seemed like no time before we were enjoying the last days of August and the start of school was just around the bend.

That year, I remember going to my secret spot and knowing it would probably be the last time I'd get to be there before we left. I walked slowly and silently through the tunnel of branches and leaves. My eyes grew big and my breath was taken away as I saw three large fish right next to my rock. I kept my distance so I could watch them move, so gracefully, through their medium. I could feel the power and the raw beauty of what I was witnessing. I thought perhaps they had come to see me off—a reward for my being a good and honest steward of the waters.

Later, I figured them to be salmon, and they were gone sooner than I'd have liked, but for me it was an early memory and an experience that I have never forgotten.

We returned home and settled back into the neighborhood. All of our friends and neighbors returned from adventures of their own. Things seamlessly flowed back to normal. Through those years we spent three or four summers at our camp, and then life got a bit more busy. My sisters were teenagers and didn't want to leave their friends, and they wanted to work summer jobs. As the years passed, we would get up there less and less often. Usually, for a night or a weekend, when the weather was too hot to bear in town. Eventually, my Dad sold that camp, leaving an empty place in my heart and reducing my childhood wonderland to fading memories.

Sometimes though, when the world is loud all around me, I can find my way back there. I can be that seven-year-old boy in 1976 sitting in his secret spot, and I can remember what I was told. That the lake has been there for a very, very long time.

Make

....

A Picnic Roll

Getting out the door for a picnic can sometimes involve a whole long list of logistics. This picnic roll was born one summer picnic season from a desire to simplify that process—in a pretty way! The simple roll is a quick sewing project that you can fill with all the utensils, napkins, and tools you need for a picnic, wherever your picnic may carry you.

SEWING NOTE

The seam allowance is ½" throughout.

WHAT YOU'LL NEED

(1) 20" x 24" piece of fabric for outer roll
(1) 20" x 24" piece of fabric for lining
(1) 20" x 24" piece of batting
(2) 12" pieces of grosgrain ribbon, lace, or bias tape for tie

WHAT TO DO

1. Place the batting on a flat surface. On top of that, place the lining fabric right side up, then place the outer fabric right

side down (so the two right sides are facing each other, with a layer of batting underneath them both). Align all sides, and pin in place.

2. Stitch around all 4 sides, leaving a 3" opening on 1 side. Trim the corners.

3. Turn the piece inside out through the 3" opening. Press. Top-stitch around all 4 sides, closing the opening in the process.

4. With the piece lying horizontally, fold the bottom edge (1 long side) up 4" to create a pocket. Pin in place. Stitch close to the edge on both sides to secure the pocket.

5. Mark with chalk or a pencil the individual pockets you would like to make for your utensils. I placed mine approximately 3" apart, leaving a larger opening for cloth napkins. Stitch over these marks to create the pocket sections, being sure to backstitch at each end.

6. Place the ends of 2 ribbons directly above the pockets you've just created on the left side of the inner fabric, about 1/2" in from the edge. Stitch in place securely.

7. Place utensils in the pockets and fold the top down to create a flap that will keep the utensils from falling out. Roll, tie, and go!

Make

....

Picnic Salads

A summer's salad is our family's favorite treat to bring along to a picnic potluck. Savoring all the flavors of the season we are in, in the presence of the natural world, is such a special treat. I asked our friend Heather Brugge-man, a fellow New Englander and wonderful cook of local, seasonal, and whole foods, to share some of her family's favorite summer salads.

Summer's Bounty Salad by Heather Bruggeman

This salad represents all things that seem to runneth over in a New England garden: zucchini, cherry tomatoes, corn, and basil. If you've never tried "raw pasta" made from fresh zucchini or raw corn fresh from the cob, now is the perfect time! Enjoy.

COOKING NOTES

It is best to combine the dressing with all of the chopped ingredients as close to serving time as possible. To make ahead, prepare the noodles, then add the other chopped veggies, nuts, and cheese in a large bowl. There is no need to even toss it all yet. Keep your dressing in a separate jar until you are ready to serve. When you're ready to eat, add the dress-ing and toss everything together gently. Perfectly fresh!

WHAT YOU'LL NEED

For the Dressing

1 teaspoon dried Italian seasoning

1 clove garlic, minced very fine

1/4 teaspoon black pepper

1/2 teaspoon sea salt

1/4 cup lemon juice

1/4 cup extra virgin olive oil

For the Salad

2 medium-sized zucchini, julienned lengthwise

3 or 4 ears fresh corn, kernels removed, or 1 1/2 cups corn

2 cups grape or cherry tomatoes, halved

1/2 cup diced red pepper

1/3 cup basil, chiffonade (stack leaves, roll, cut into long ribbons)

1/2 cup roughly chopped walnuts or pine nuts

4 ounces feta cheese, crumbled or diced small

Sea salt for sprinkling on zucchini

WHAT TO DO

1. Whisk all dressing ingredients together, or just combine them in a jar with a screw top lid and give it a good shake. Set the dressing aside at least 30 minutes for flavors to develop.

2. Next, prepare the zucchini "noodles." (If you happen to have a spiralizer, that would be the tool to use; some folks use a serrated vegetable peeler. I use a simple chef's knife

so I will give instructions for that. It takes a little longer this way, but I love a few quiet minutes in the kitchen.) Slice off the ends of the zucchini, then slice off a very thin piece lengthwise. This will give you a flat surface to rest the zucchini on while you continue to slice it lengthwise, creating very thin (yet wide) sections. Lay those sections flat on your cutting board and slice them thinly (lengthwise) again, creating long noodlelike pieces. Place the zucchini in a bowl, sprinkle it lightly with sea salt, and gently toss it to move the salt around. Cover the bowl, and place it in the refrigerator for 30 minutes. The salt draws moisture out of the zucchini making the noodles soft and pastalike.

3. In a large mixing bowl, gently combine the drained zucchini noodles, dressing, and the rest of the ingredients. Serve.

Farmer's Market Salad by Heather Bruggeman
This salad was born three years ago from a need to be fed simply and quickly. My family has spent many summer weekends beside me as I displayed and sold my handmade wares at our local farmer's market. We loved coming home to this simple, nourishing meal, collecting most of the ingredients throughout the day from our market neighbors.

COOKING NOTES

Lemon balm is a member of the mint family and is a low maintenance, pretty perennial to include in your herb garden. The tender leaves are tasty and calming in iced tea, and the stems of lemon balm make a fragrant addition to your cut flower arrangements.

WHAT YOU'LL NEED

For the Dressing
1/8 cup extra virgin olive oil
1/8 cup balsamic vinaigrette
1/8 cup water
1 tablespoon maple syrup (agave nectar or honey are fine to use)
1 tablespoon Country Dijon mustard (coarse ground)
Sea salt and black pepper to taste

For the Salad
6–8 cups fresh salad greens of your choice
1 cup pecans
1$^1/_2$ tablespoons maple syrup (or honey)
A sprinkle of sea salt

8–10 fresh strawberries, tops removed and sliced

4 ounces fresh goat cheese (chèvre, herbed if you like), sliced thin

1/4 cup fresh lemon balm (or any bright flavored fresh herb), chopped fine

WHAT TO DO

1. Whisk together the dressing ingredients, or combine and shake them in a lidded glass jar. Set the mixture aside for 10 minutes.

2. Make the maple-glazed pecans. In a skillet over medium to medium high heat, toast the pecans for 3–5 minutes, stirring often. Sprinkle with a small pinch of sea salt. Once they are nicely toasted (don't let them burn!), add the maple syrup. Immediately turn the heat down to medium to medium low, stirring often for another minute or so. Again, watch carefully so they do not burn. They will still feel sticky to the touch, but don't worry. Remove them from the heat, and allow them to cool. I turn the pecans out onto a dinner plate, and they cool quickly in a single layer. They will become drier to the touch as they cool.

3. The salad can be arranged as one large family style salad or individually on 4 plates if you prefer. Either way, simply nestle the salad greens into a large shallow serving dish. Follow by arranging the following ingredients evenly over the top: sliced strawberries, sliced chèvre, fresh herb, and pecans. Pass the dressing at the table.

Da
....

Have a Picnic

Family picnics are so special to us, and I know they have been for generations and generations before. There's something magical about trans-
porting an everyday family meal into the outdoors—whether it be at the
beach, in the woods, in a desert, or at the park. That's the beauty of it—
that fun outdoor picnic spots can be found anywhere and everywhere,
even your backyard!

Sometimes our picnics are planned far in advance with friends or
around a special date. But my favorite kinds of picnics might just be the
impromptu ones. The picnics that come about after a long day of work
and play—these kinds of picnics where we quite literally hop in the car
(or on a bike or trail!) and go. The spontaneous adventures like these
become favorite surprises for my little ones and treasured memories for
me as a Mama.

Of course, "hopping in the car to go" is what the little ones do. But
gathering a meal does take a bit of planning on the adults' part. I like to
keep our picnic basket ready to go and stocked full of the essential supplies, so that when inspiration strikes, I can simply add the food and hop
in the car right behind the kids!

Here are some tips for making the most of your family picnic time.

1. Baby powder or dusting talc works wonderfully for removing a bit of sand before eating or on the way home.

2. Wet sacks—bags for putting wet clothes and towels in—are tremendously helpful in keeping all the damp, wet clothes together upon leaving a spot.

3. Glass jars—Mason or Ball canning jars, or peanut butter and condiment jars—are excellent food containers for traveling. The thick glass doesn't break easily, and with the many sizes available, you can find one just right for what you need without wasting precious space in your picnic bag!

4. Enamelware is my favorite outdoor dishware material. It's often found at thrift shops or otherwise inexpensively. Hard, vintage melamine (remember Melmac?) is another favorite, preferred over the softer contemporary plastic.

THE ESSENTIAL ALWAYS-PACKED CHECKLIST

Bag for garbage or compost to bring home
Bottle opener
Bag for dishes and returnables (reusable, drawstring poly bags are
  wonderful for this!)
Bowls (I find bowls to be easier at picnics and on laps than plates!)
Bread knife
Cups
Flatware
Napkins for everyone, plus some extra
Spreading knife

5. To eliminate the need for disposable flatware while also saving your silverware for inside the house, consider looking at thrift stores and yard sales for random, mismatched pieces of flatware especially reserved for use at picnics and such.
6. Bring more water than you think you will need!
7. Remember to put your picnic essentials right back in their roll (see A Picnic Roll on page 117) after cleaning them at home so they're ready to go next time the picnic inspiration strikes!

July

Follow Them

I've always loved watching our oldest—and not-so-little-any-more—boy of mine solve problems. He's persistent, focused, creative, and determined in whatever path he's on. It isn't often that he wants my help these days making things—at least not in the same way he used to. Such is growing up . . . and being quite capable of making things on his own. So on those occasions when he does ask for such help, I'm quite grateful for the chance to give it.

Coming home, smelling of wood smoke from a weekend camping trip (oh, that smell is heavenly), he told me he needed "something to carry my pocketknife in." Apparently, just putting it in his pocket wasn't working for him anymore. So the next day he worked on a few ideas of his own. The always-useful cardboard and duct tape, elastic and fabric. He was on a daylong search for just the right thing. After a few goes that didn't quite get him where he wanted, Calvin finally came to me and announced, "I need the sewing machine."

Indeed, he did. And so he proceeded to work out the kinks of just what he needed—how big it should be, how it would fold over his belt, what kind of fabric would be best. I offered advice when asked, and I gave a few suggestions, some of which he kindly ignored ("No embroidery embellishment? Are you sure?") and some he warmly embraced.

In no time at all with some stitching and cutting and snap-setting, he had just the right pouch he was after. After a day's worth of work and all that problem solving, he gave a quiet, satisfied "huh!" to himself with a smile. A quick "thanks, Mom!" and then he was out the door. Out the door to whittle another spoon, or make another tool, or add a piece to his growing fort. Out the door to discover something new.

Children are so curious. They want to understand the world around them, they try with all of their might to make sense of it: to find out how things work, what effect they have on their environment, and how they can shape things. But their curious exploration expands beyond their imaginations—they explore with every one of their senses. They want to see the world, taste it, touch it, smell it. And in this way, they do come to understand and know it—not just with their minds but with their whole bodies. Their confidence is inspiring. Their abilities unending. There is much we can learn from the way our children experience the world around them.

Frances Hodgson Burnett wrote, "The secret garden is always open now. Open, and awake, and alive. If you look the right way, you can see that the whole world is a garden." Indeed, children are very aware of this. And when we follow them, when we watch that and take part in it ourselves, we can discover the very miracles that they discover.

Upon returning home from the grocery market recently, with kids in tow, bags and bags full of food, and dinner long overdue, I start to haul myself and our bags up the stairs to our home. The dialog of what's for dinner, what time baseball practice begins, and so on begins in vigor. Ezra, my six-year-old, stops in his tracks on the way up the stairs and holds out his hands for us all to stop behind him. "Stop!" he says. "A frog! The biggest frog in the whole world!"

Grocery bags are dropped, children run, and the frog is instantly surrounded by an audience the likes of which it has never experienced. One runs for a field book to identify the exact frog, the other runs to find a leaf to "feed" the frog. Just at that moment, we hear a flurry in the woods and I look up to spy two pileated woodpeckers. As bird lovers, we've only seen these birds twice in our eight years of living in this city home of ours. Before I know what's happened, we are led on a chase through the woods, quietly tiptoeing behind them as they flitter from tree to tree.

Dinner is forgotten. We opt for popcorn. And over that popcorn, the wonder of what we've seen takes place. My daughter remembers what the frog felt like when she held it in her hands. Calvin remembers how quiet it was in the woods. Ezra remembers how loud the woodpeckers were against the tree. I remember the sight of all three of them staring in awe.

At the end of the day tucking my little one into bed, she declares, "That was an *amazing* day. We saw two pileated woodpeckers, the biggest frog in the whole world, and a ladybug! What a lucky day!" A lucky day— just like every other day—indeed. These amazing days are out there truly every single day, should we choose to stop and love them. Just like the little ones do so very well in their own curious and exploring ways.

PAPA

A Child's Game

On my eleventh birthday, I got a new baseball glove. I recall my Dad saying, "If you take care of it, you'll have that glove forever." I worked it, oiled it, tied a ball inside it, and sat on the back steps just throwing into the palm to break it in right. Day after day I played until, eventually, the leather began to soften and it closed automatically, with a slap, every time. After the season, when the weather cooled and my interest shifted to other pursuits, I put it on the shelf. There it sat, patiently awaiting the next opportunity to slip into action and perform. Occasionally, over the long winter, I would take it to the basement and bounce a ball off the concrete foundation. I would act out fictitious games in my mind, playing alongside my heroes of the day. Imagining myself as the hero, I would play for hours on end.

Every spring, as baseball season rolled around again, I took the field with my old glove. I was considerably larger and the balls came much faster, but to me, it was still a child's game. I called on the skills I learned as a boy to serve me as a young man. I remember how strange it was to play my last game as an almost 18-year-old and wonder what my life would be like without playing baseball. By the time college came around, my glove spent most of its year in the closet. I became more interested in paddling and biking and other gravity sports that didn't require me to field a team. When I started to travel, the glove went into my Mom's attic and stayed there for many years. Baseball was part of my past.

By the time my first child, Calvin, turned six, he was throwing hard enough for me to dig my old glove out of the bag and use it once again. A flood of memories returned to me as that familiar sound of the popping mitt resonated in my ear. My own child before me, entranced with the discovery of a new game and the ability with which he could play, gleaming with excitement, as I did so long ago. Now I have four children at play. Sometimes the game is baseball, where the grass gets worn to dirt from the patterns of their steps. Other times it is tag or hide and seek or games they have learned and need to teach me the rules of before we play. Regardless of the activity, I watch them play and I am transformed back into the mind of a playful child.

These days we spend a good portion of each spring at the ball field with the kids and their friends, playing, watching, coaching them along. As summer comes and goes and the leagues wind down, the fields empty out and sit dormant until the following spring. All the gloves, including mine, are put away for the season. For me, it is bittersweet, showing me the connection to my children through the mutual love of a game and the passing of another year of their childhood, wanting to hold them in my arms and keep them here forever where I can protect them and watch them play their games. I remember how eager I was at eleven to grow up. A life of possibilities and excitement spread out before me. I look at my old glove, the leather worn completely through the pocket from the constant pounding of a lifetime of games. Playing catch with my Dad and my best friend and all my teammates over the years, and now, my own children.

When my Dad comes to visit, the kids pull his old glove out from their gear bag where they keep it safe for him. It is even more tattered and beaten and loved than mine, and again I hear his words from my birthday so long ago, "If you take care of it, you'll have that glove forever."

Make

....

Bug Stay-Away

Of course, there really is no magic cure for keeping the bugs at bay—they are present in our seasons and an important part of our ecosystem (as my little ones remind me). That doesn't mean, however, that we want them biting us to bits! A little spray of repellent helps to keep them away just a little more, and us outside just a little more. But products loaded with potentially harmful chemicals on your skin and the skin of your little ones might not be the answer you're looking for either. We like to make our own simple insect repellent, particularly geared toward keeping away those mosquitoes and black flies found so often in the early summer months here in Maine. We find this simple concoction works well for us and, most especially, for keeping us safe and smelling good upon our return home inside from the bug-filled woods!

WHAT YOU'LL NEED

1 teaspoon lemongrass oil
1 teaspoon eucalyptus oil
1 teaspoon citronella oil
7 ounces witch hazel
8-ounce spray bottle

WHAT TO DO

Mix all the ingredients in the spray bottle. Shake well before each use. Apply lightly to skin, avoiding contact with eyes, nose, and mouth. Reapply as desired, every hour or so. Will keep for a season.

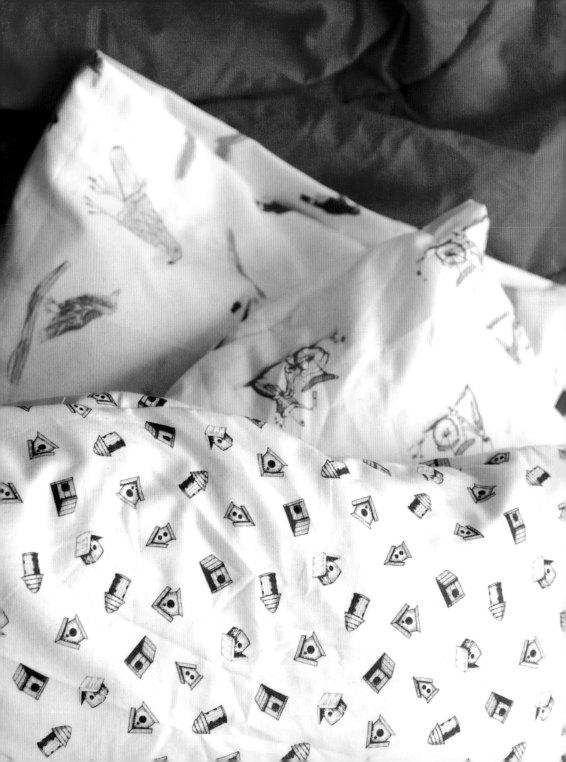

Make

....

Sweet Dreams Camp Pillow and Case

There's no better way to truly experience all that the outside world has to offer than to rest your head and sleep under the stars. This pillow will give a little bit of the comfort of your own bed in a portable camp size and features a removable pillowcase that's made for washing over and over. To make it extra special, choose a fabric for your pillowcase that has meaning to you. Our pillowcase fabric features hand-drawn birds that my little ones sketched. A dear friend of mine tried this pattern out as a going away gift for her college-aged daughter, making the pillow from one of her father's dress shirts. Her daughter embroidered it with their favorite camp memories.

SEWING NOTES

The seam allowance is 1/2" except as noted.

A soft cotton works best for this project, both for the pillow and the case. Remember that it will be next to the skin! The pillow fabric is a great way to repurpose nearly any fabric you might not have another need for, as it won't be seen often.

Bamboo works best for the pillow stuffing; it has a natural antibacterial element, is ecologically sound, and feels good against the skin. It can also be machine washed as necessary.

The pillowcase calls for a French seam, which will eliminate any raw edges from showing along the seams of your pillowcase.

WHAT YOU'LL NEED

(2) 14" x 19" pieces for the pillow
(1) 15" x 44" piece for the pillowcase
Fiberfill, approximately 10 ounces

WHAT TO DO

1. Place the 2 pieces of pillow fabric right sides together. Beginning in the middle of a short (14") side, stitch around all 4 sides, stopping 3" before your starting point to leave an opening. Trim the corners, and turn it right side out.

2. Using small handfuls of fill at a time, insert fill into the opening. Fill the pillow completely, but do not overstuff it. When the pillow is full to your liking, close the 3" opening by using a zigzag stitch. (This will be on the inside of your pillowcase and not seen.)

3. For the pillowcase, fold your fabric in half, wrong sides together, so that it measures 15" x 22". You'll now create a French seam as follows: With a 1/8" seam allowance stitch down the long side of the case. Repeat on the opposite side. Trim the excess fabric as close to the stitches as you can without cutting them. Turn the pillowcase wrong side out, and press the seams. Now, using a 5/8" seam allowance, stitch down the length of 1 side. Repeat for the second side.

4. Keeping the pillowcase wrong side out, fold the open edge of the pillowcase over 1/4". Press. Fold again 1" and press. Edge stitch this seam in place.

5. Turn the pillowcase right side out and insert your pillow, zigzag stitch first, into the pillowcase.

Make

....

Summer Smoothies

Our family has become huge fans of green smoothies all year round. But it was at the height of the summer growing season—when the abundance of green, fresh foods fills up our refrigerator shelves—that the love for them began. Smoothies are such a wonderful way to use all those last bits of freshness provided for us in our gardens or at our local markets. They're a wonderful cool-me-down and pick-me-up at the same time. And frankly, they offer the best way I know to get raw, fresh greens into the tummy of any little eater. The variations for smoothies are as endless as there are fruits and vegetables available to you to try. This recipe is provided merely as a starting point for you to play with, tweak, and enjoy to your family's summer content!

WHAT YOU'LL NEED

1 (packed) cup dark greens, chopped (kale, chard, spinach, romaine, and so on)

1 cup tree fruit, sliced (pears, apples, oranges, and so on— keep the skin on!)

1 cup berries (strawberries, blueberries, raspberries, and so on)

1 tablespoon honey

1 cup ice cubes

$1/2$ cup water, or more as needed to blend thoroughly

WHAT TO DO

Place all the ingredients in a blender and blend until mixed. Pour and serve!

Smoothies can be refrigerated for later in the day. Most blenders will not be able to make a creamy consistency from the leafy greens, but that's okay! You may find (as we do) that you like the consistency and "bits of chewy green," as my kids say.

Smoothies are also a wonderful place to include any supplements you wish to incorporate into your diet, without tasting them much—such as cod liver oil, flax seed oil, and the like. (And the good news: smoothies aren't just for summer!)

Do

....

Go Camping

Some of my own favorite childhood memories are of time spent camping with my family. Free from the distractions of our daily lives, I felt so thrilled to have the complete and undivided attention of my parents! Not to mention the most wonderful playground in the world—the trees and shore and landscape of wherever we happened to be camping at the moment. I never understood as a child, of course, just how much went into getting all six of us out the door and comfortably into the woods for days at a time. It seemed such a seamless task. But as a parent now, with my own family of six, I know that the reality is otherwise.

To be successful with kids, a good camping trip takes a proper amount of planning and organizing. There's nothing like getting to your wilderness destination and being completely ill prepared for what lies there—with little ones in tow. We've had our share of ups and downs as we've worked out just what we need and how to get out the door in my family. It's a delicate balance between wanting to be sure you've packed enough of what you'll need, and enjoying the very simplicity and easy days that you went camping for in the first place!

Involving your children in the process—from packing to planning your days—is an essential part of a successful trip. Following are a few things to keep in mind as you plan for your family's foray into the wonderful world of wilderness camping.

1. Lists are your friend! Regardless of whether you're a regular list maker or not, in this instance, I encourage you to create one! Begin a packing list well in advance of your trip so there is plenty of time to add things as you get closer to the date. Involve your children in the process. Have them help check things off when they are ready to go. If they are old enough, have them make their own packing list!

2. Keep your plans realistic. Ease yourself and your children into the experience! Try a small camping trip—maybe just one or two nights—before heading out on a weeklong expedition with your little ones. Backyard camping might be a great way to try everything out (including your gear!), and car camping—perhaps near running water—might be especially helpful for those who are new to or skeptical of camping in the woods.

3. Don't overdo it! Look for used gear, borrow from friends, or check thrift shops (this is where I get all of our camping kitchenware!). Keep the values of respecting and loving the earth in mind as you prepare for your trip as well by avoiding excess and waste.

4. Keep a bit of your home routine. For many little ones, routine is so very important in the smoothness of their days. If you normally read stories after brushing your teeth before bed, try to make that happen while camping. If a nap or quiet time usually occurs in your afternoon, try to do the same while in the woods. This will help your little ones feel secure and allow them to explore comfortably!

5. Plan on layering. (And obviously pack only clothes that you don't mind getting dirty. How unfortunate for a child to be in the woods and be told not to get his or her clothes dirty!)

6. Include the kids *and* the adults equally in the experience. Though that's already been said, it can't be stated enough. Be sure your kids have their own flashlights. Let them help when it comes to planning how you'll spend your days. Give them a journal or camera to document their own experience.

7. Have a backup plan. Both for unexpected weather, and also for illness or temperament. Give yourself and your children the freedom to try it again another time, without pressure or shame at how your experience has gone. Each trip is a learning experience, which makes the next one even better.

8. Roll with it. Be flexible. You *will* forget something; it's inevitable. It's also part of the fun, part of the experience! My children like to tease me about the time I forgot all of our spoons and forks. We had knives and pots and pans, but nothing to eat with! Naturally, the kids decided to take it upon themselves to remedy the situation—by making chopsticks out of the woods around us!

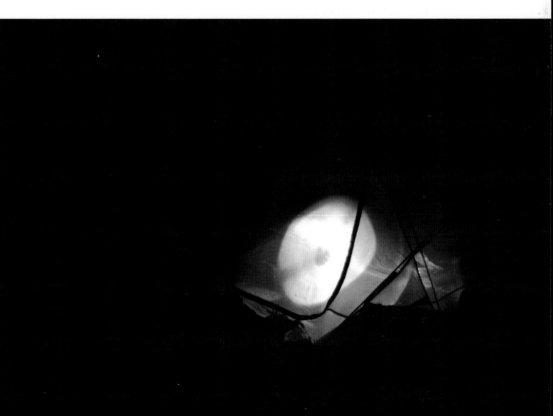

August

Submerge

I have loved watching each of my children begin a relationship with the ocean. There are so many childlike similarities in their discovery— the fascination, the exploration, and all from the safe arms of a parent. But beyond a few similarities, they have each approached it and subsequently fallen in love in a way that is uniquely their own. I watch Calvin study the waves, analyzing how he'll navigate a board over them. It's the same way he watched them and studied them closely as a two-year-old. My son Ezra dances with the waves. For as long as I can remember, each beach trip would involve him running as fast as he could for the shore, immersing himself in the waves and singing and dancing with a fierce and beautiful energy I love. Adelaide submerges herself in the water, completely comfortable under it, coming up for air with such glee on her face that cannot be replicated. And now, I watch as Harper begins his own relationship with the water—tentative, curious, and a little bit excited. I cannot wait to see what he does.

One of the beauties of the beach for me is that there is "nothing" to do and, of course, "everything" to do at the very same time. We begin our beach days early in the morning, with snacks prepared as everyone gets ready, and the beach bag perpetually packed beside the door. There is nothing that elicits such a rush and smooth transition out of the door as the call of "We're going to the beach! Bathing suits *on!*"

We arrive at the beach full of excitement, energy, and clean towels.

A blanket is spread out, sun block applied, sun hats adjusted, shoes long gone . . . And there, for the day, we are. We just are. We swim, we laugh, we play ball, we snack, we read, we explore, we have many moments of quiet and stillness. All from the home base of a three-foot-square blanket. So very much happens on those days of nothing at the shore. So very much living happens there.

It's one of the most important lessons I think we can give our children: An appreciation and love of being still. Frequent days when there is no schedule, no plan, no rushing about from here to there.

It's about the art of being where you are. The ability to sit at the shore—to explore, with only one's imagination, the tools of the earth, and sometimes each other. I do believe this is the kind of lesson and gift that will continue to nurture their spirits for the rest of their lives: When they are able to find quiet in the middle of our busy lives. When they are able to sit under a tree and just think, just dream, just be for all the time that they need. These are essential lessons of childhood that will carry them into peaceful, healthy adults, able to find peace and quiet amidst the busy days and lives that we all ultimately lead. The outside world has a healing power—showing them that fact at a young age is giving them a lifelong gift of the way to a peaceful heart.

I think of these things along the shore as I watch my children play. As I play, I too find restorative peace from the deep breaths and the ocean waves. It reminds me that I want to savor these days, to sink into them, to say yes to every beach day that I realistically can. I want to pick, eat, and love every tomato, cucumber, or bean that might yet grow. I want to drop everything and just *go* whenever there is a call for evening picnics, music by the lake, beachside gatherings, berry picking adventures, poolside fun, forest jaunts, friendly barbecues, and nights spent under the stars. I will, with all of my heart, say *yes* to all of that—savoring the bounty and beauty of the summer. I want to submerge myself in all that this place has to share with me.

I have a growing tradition these past years of taking a sunset swim on my birthday. It falls late in the summer, and it's a cold ocean, but it's a wonderful one. We often find ourselves alone at the beach that late in the year and that late in the day. But there we are. This year, I take my swim with my littlest baby, Harper, just about a year old. There is no fear or worry; he knows he is safe in my arms. Standing beside him, holding his hand, I watch as a wave approaches. It is enough to knock him over and wash the water over his head for a moment. But I haven't let go. And when the wave subsides, he looks up at me with the widest eyes and just a bit of shock on his face. He sees me, and just a second later, a huge smile crosses his face as the surge of the ocean's energy hits him.

It's familiar. I know that feeling. The feeling of being submerged in the cold ocean. It's like nothing else—a sudden, powerful, and joyful reminder of being completely and fully alive.

We Belong Here

We sit with our feet in the water, taking in the sounds of a summer afternoon: The waves lap against the dock and shore. The breeze beginning to stiffen a bit. The kids reeling in their lines and casting again. I can see clouds gathering in the distance and wonder if we are due for some weather to roll through later in the day. The sun melts away any tension as I shift from pulling weeds off one lure to untangling a second, only to repeat the process in another minute. It's a rare moment of unified contentment and serenity amongst siblings. No big needs, no complaints, not even a rambling story unfurling to which I must pay attention or risk failing the ensuing quiz. Just a peaceful moment floating by on a midsummer day.

"Listen to the trees blowing in that breeze," I mention with my eye to the sky.

"Huh. That's really loud," says Calvin.

"Yeah . . . that is loud."

I look back to the gathering clouds, which have rapidly halved the distance between us and darkened considerably. "That storm is rolling in pretty fast," I say.

They, paying little attention to what lurks on the horizon, continue about the business at hand: fishing. I, however, am now realizing this is an impending situation about to unfold.

"Look!!" I point to the treetops across the water, which are swaying as if being shaken from below. "You can see the rain coming!"

The kids, feeling the energy swarm around them, start to dance around the dock. Laughing. Continuing to fish.

"Papa!! It's raining!!" exclaims Adelaide as if this is the first she's heard of it.

"Watch it come!!" I yell above the roar of the tumult.

The far side of the lake begins to turn over and boil from the pounding.

The rain drops continue to hit us, fat drops, coming in at a rapidly increasing pace. They fall with an audible slap upon the wooden dock.

"Should we run for camp?" they ask.

"Either that or wait it out . . . and get really wet!!"

Screaming and laughing we opt to head for cover and watch the show from inside. Darting down the trail with shirts and towels over our heads the storm engulfs us, fierce, heavy rain coming down straight and hard. Giggling we break through the door where Mama greets us with warm joy and the promise of special comforts to fit such an occasion. Snacks and drinks are prepared as we start to strip down and head for dry clothes. "I want to go for a paddle!!" Calvin declares, while staring out the window at the action.

For a brief moment my heart sinks as I feel the warm hold of the immediate surroundings begin to slip. Then my eyes alight.

"Yes!!"

We scamper to the shed to grab paddles and jackets. Working together we turn over the canoe and slide it into the cove, the trees providing us a small measure of protection from the onslaught above. Calvin hops nimbly into the bow and I shove off and step aboard.

His gaze affixed on the rocky path to open water, we stroke easy for a minute until we clear the obstacles. Our rhythm quickly falls in tune, and we are out in it.

Calvin paddles, strong and athletic, with his head up.

The storm continues to dump rain in a torrent. The drops careening into the lake in sheets, juxtaposing a soft blanket of sound against the hard drive of the elements. We shift sides without talking and move quickly across the surface of the lake into a narrow channel with steep granite banks falling away to a deep water abyss.

My heart swells with gratitude for the moment.

For decades I have paddled a host of watercraft down rivers and creeks, across lakes and seas, into the depths of the canyons and in the shadows of the mountains. Countless evenings, putting the sun to rest from the cockpit of my boat. Waking with the sunrise for another day afloat. Never have I been more moved by the wonder of nature than when paddling with my son across this ancient lake, carved over millions of years by glaciers and rains such as this.

He turns to make eye contact for the first time since we shoved off.

"This was a good idea," I say.

Smiling he turns back around.

We belong here.

Make

....

Berry Muffins

Late in summer in Maine, we are often in an abundance of berries. Blueberries, late strawberries, raspberries, blackberries, and more. Jams are made, berries are frozen, and smoothies are devoured for breakfast and lunch. And there are always, always berry muffins! I freeze the berries in amounts just right for this recipe, so we can enjoy the summer berry treats all winter long.

COOKING NOTES

Coconut oil is a good saturated fat. I use it often as a replacement for oil and butter in recipes. (It's also great on your skin!) Coconut oil should be stored at room temperature. It's important to note that the other ingredients should also be at room temperature when cooking with coconut oil or it will solidify. (If this does happen, don't worry; just keep stirring! It will taste just right.)

WHAT YOU'LL NEED

$1/2$ cup coconut oil, melted (vegetable oil is an
 alternative option)
$1/3$ cup maple syrup or honey
1 teaspoon pure vanilla extract

2 large eggs
1 cup unbleached flour
1 cup whole wheat pastry flour
1 teaspoon baking powder
$^1/_2$ teaspoon salt
1$^1/_2$ cups any combination of available berries,
  cut if necessary

WHAT TO DO

Mix the dry ingredients in a large bowl. Mix the wet
  ingredients separately. Add the wet ingredients to the
  dry, and stir until combined. Gently fold in the berries.
Spoon the batter into a greased muffin pan. Bake at 350°F
  for 30 minutes or until a tester comes out clean. Let the
  muffins cool in the pan for 10 minutes, then remove them
  to a baking rack until you are ready to eat. These muffins
  can be stored in an airtight container for 2 days (but are
  best eaten right away!).
Optional: Sprinkle dark brown or raw sugar on top of the
  muffins before baking for an extra sweet treat!

Make

....

A Muffin Bag

These drawstring linen bags are the solution I came up with for storing breads, crackers, and muffins without the use of disposable plastic or paper. I love them for keeping baked goods fresh at home and for traveling with to picnics and outings. And there's nothing greater than giving them as a gift—stuffed full of a fresh batch of Berry Muffins (see page 155).

SEWING NOTES

The seam allowance is ½" throughout.

Any linen, hemp, or breathable broadcloth cotton will work well for the bag's fabric. I love using vintage tea towels—they're usually just the right size, and it's the perfect use for such an old treat to be seen so visibly like this. The tea towel fabric is usually just perfect for storing food.

WHAT YOU'LL NEED

(2) 11" x 13" pieces of fabric for the bag
30" piece of ribbon, bias binding, or twine for the drawstring, not wider than ½"
Seam ripper

WHAT TO DO

1. Place the 2 pieces of fabric for the bag right sides together. Stitch around both long sides and the bottom.

2. Finish the seams by using a zigzag stitch over your seam allowance (in the space between the stitches and the raw edge of the fabric). Stop 2" before the open top end on each side. This finishing will help keep the inside fabric seam from fraying onto your food. The top 2" are reserved for the drawstring casing later.

3. Keep the bag wrong side out and fold down the top edge $1/2$" to the wrong side. Press. Fold again by 1" and press again. Edge stitch in place.

4. Turn the bag right side out. Machine stitch another row of stitching around the entire top edge, $1/8$" from the top, reinforcing by backstitching at the side seams. You've now created a casing at the top in which to insert your drawstring.

5. On 1 outside seam, in the casing area you just created, use a seam ripper to open the side seam in the casing area only.

6. Place a large safety pin in the end of your chosen drawstring tie, and insert it through the opening you just created. Pull it through and around the entire bag, exiting from the same spot you entered. Remove the safety pin and tie a knot at both ends of the drawstring to keep it from slipping inside the casing.

Da

....

Treasure Nature

Naturalists—young and old alike—are bound to be living amongst collections: collections of rocks, feathers, acorns, pine cones, leaves, and other bits of nature that call and speak to us. Bringing these things inside to enjoy extends our time examining the elements of nature and allows us to think more upon the role these things play in our natural world. Once inside, so much more can be done with them, as they beckon our attention and draw our imagination closer with endless possibility for play, craft, and dreaming.

There are, of course, some guidelines to follow when collecting pieces of the earth. Keep in mind the rules of the area you are visiting. Limit your takings to the minimum. It needn't be every single time you are out that a treasure comes home with you. You want to experience your moments spent outdoors together without the promise or habit of always taking something with you. But once in a while, if something really speaks to you, or if you are hoping to mark a momentous trip or expedition, this is the time to do so.

There are endless possibilities when it comes to storing and displaying your collected nature bits. You'll see a few of our favorites scattered through the images in this book: vintage tins, glass jars, wooden bowls, tea cups, wooden boxes and crates, an open shelf, planters, baskets, and Tiny Felted Treasure Bowls (see page 53). Another favorite spot for displaying bits of nature might be your garden! A shell, some rocks, a few special sticks here and there can really shine in a space of growth.

Once you are safely past the age of worry with toddlers and choking hazards, it's important that the bits of nature your family collects be made accessible to little hands for touching, exploring, and remembering. Whether this is done in small amounts or with an entire collection is up to you and your children. We often rotate in and out a few of our favorite things seasonally or otherwise, like leaving out a bowl full of acorns and some empty space on which little ones can touch, arrange, play with, and display to their heart's content. Other things—our bowl full of heart-shaped rocks, for example—are always out and present in our family living space. I like to think of these little bits of collected earth as tools and materials for creating art. I believe this touch with natural materials—well beyond the moments of actually being outside gathering them—further serves to create a connection to the world around us. Think of a basket of rocks as a basket of blocks or other building materials for your young learners. The art materials of the earth are really the finest of tools and loveliest of toys. They are our gifts from the earth.

September

I Dream of Tomatoes

When I grow up I want to be a tomato farmer. Sure, I grow them now. I grow them amidst many other vegetables and herbs that my family can eat, in a garden that is quite happily balanced to nourish those in my care. Vegetable gardening is a love and also a chosen necessity. But someday, when these children of mine are grown up just a little bit, I want to grow just tomatoes. I want to have a garden full of as many different varieties of tomatoes as it will hold: brandywine, cherry, sungold, Juliet, pink beauties, grape, black prince, Oregon spring, and so many more I have yet to know. I pour over their names in the seed catalogs and they roll off my tongue over and over as I dream about them.

I dream in red during tomato season.

The plants grow so slowly and steadily all season long. From seeds in the last days of snow they are nurtured from the very beginning with water, sun, and great care. The seedlings make their way outside when they are strong enough and the warmth has hit the ground. We weed around them, we cultivate them, we watch them grow. As the green tomatoes make their appearance, we watch carefully—for signs of blight, for too much water. We take great care. A season goes by.

Just as our summer season is coming to an end, they blossom. First just one early tomato is red—and surely there is nothing tastier than the first tomato of the year, right off the plant. It's a gift that should always be shared with the youngest in our clan in our home and garden, a true treasure from the harvest. Then, there are so many more to come. More pop each day, as we bring them in to ripen, to eat, to share with those we love, and to put by for seasons to come. Before we know it, we are in abundance of these precious tomatoes—they are piled in bowls and on every counter available in our little kitchen. We make sauce, salsa, paste. Tomatoes are stewed and boiled. Frozen and canned. For that very short period of time when we are so blessed with a good crop, the tomatoes just keep coming. We finish boiling and peeling and preparing and canning, then turn our back to find another bowl full—waiting for the same. The kitchen and my mind are full of tomatoes. Tomatoes line the windowsills getting just that last bit of sun to ripen. Skins fill our overflowing kitchen compost bucket that I am quite certain we just took out. Tomato seeds stick to my apron. A red juice lines the countertops. Our fingers are now stained red, and the dreams commence.

There's something so wonderful about such a short harvest season— one that can produce so very much in such a short period of time. A harvest that will yield the kinds of food my family will eat and enjoy all the year long, until the next one comes. In the weeks that the tomatoes are in abundance like this, it becomes my much-loved, full-time job to preserve them. We have only a matter of days to do so, and these days are spent so fully absorbed in the work of one thing. One simple vegetable that consumes our days and our work until the task is done. It's an exercise in mindfulness that I treasure each year. As I think of the wonder of this magical seasonal offering, I feel full. It is a time full of appreciation for the glorious abundance we are given in one simple, beautiful, perfect, round red fruit.

I think about these things as I am peeling tomatoes with my children in the kitchen. As my youngest toddler rides a tricycle between my legs and around the kitchen island, as I remind my oldest to take off his cleats before walking into the kitchen. I know this food will feed these growing loves of mine all winter long, and I love that. Then my mind wanders to years from now. Years, perhaps, when Steve and I are alone, and I am wandering quietly through the rows and rows of tomato plants, caring, nurturing, and sharing them with those I love.

Labor Day

It's Labor Day weekend and we're gathering again to close out another summer. Closest friends, their children, their pets, and us in a spot of wilderness we hold dear. For some this is a relaxing journey into the heart of what they most cherish. For others, it's a stretch of what they consider "comfortably away" from the civilized world. Once all have arrived, we sink into family and all that is outside drifts away as we turn our smiling faces to the late summer breeze.

The children do not wait to break free with overflowing joy at the possibilities this place holds for them: The moss covered rocks in a secret trickling stream that meanders quietly past and holds frogs and salamanders and tadpoles. The forest looming large and mysterious, its floor covered in pine needles and strewn with chunks of granite, its canopy allowing light to pass in a myriad of dizzying shapes and shades. Their whole world alive with the buzz of life in the trees. The allure of the water takes over, and they plunge in a host of disjointed shapes into its depths. Connecting. Sinking into that which is their very being. Water.

Their styles, as diverse as their personalities, glimmer in the afternoon sun. Cautiously deliberate, recklessly carefree, daringly calculated, whimsically unaware. The raw beauty of the land speckled liberally with vibrant human energy. They are flowers.

Adults breathe in the air and rejoice in the glory of time without persistent responsibility. Fires are tended, meals prepared, children enjoyed. We move slowly. We laugh often.

We gather and the conversations spark and run together and ring across the water. We sit beneath the stars and ponder our small part as the fire crackles and dances to the delight of us all. I take the moment to watch it all unfold. I look at my own children and see them growing before my eyes. I watch them interact with their friends and other adults, and I am amazed and proud. I listen to Calvin spin a story for a group of people, and as they laugh and joke and fuel his spirit, I just stare, mesmerized, and watch a boy who will one day be a man.

I listen to Adelaide and Ezra talk like friends as he helps her find "just the right stick" with which to toast marshmallows. Their shyness fading away amongst so many friends, they open up and answer questions and act like themselves.

I see Amanda's face beaming in the flickering light. Her smile is full, our baby asleep in her arms. I see the woman whom I will accompany on the journey into old age. When these babies have grown and the quiet of night descends, it will be her hand in mine.

The mood turns to melancholy as our time away comes to an end. Our friends scatter off to make their own way home. I comb the waterfront one last time to check for things left behind. What I find are the echoes of laughter and play that we sprinkled along the hillside, fresh footprints worn into an old, winding trail.

A ripple across the cove splashes ashore, barely audible.

With some regret that I have to leave a place such as this, I turn and make my way back down that familiar twisting path.

Make

....

Harvest Notes

I find it so helpful to record my Harvest Notes from year to year. There are so many details that I think I could never forget, but I always end up doing so. Remembering what I planted, how much, and where. Remembering the yield that such planting produced, and just what it was I made with that yield. Remembering how many jars of jam and jelly I made this year and then how long into the year they lasted. All of these are helpful in planning the next year's garden and make for a better gardening experience for me—one that produces what my family needs.

I like to keep a book for each year, for which I make and use the Nature Notebook found on page 79. Here are some things I include in the pages.

Seeds ordered—from where and when, and how much
When the garden was planted
Where various crops were planted in our garden
Struggles we had through the year (blight, drought, groundhogs)
Approximate yield
Favorite recipes used for that harvest
How much of each crop was put by for the season to come
When the pantry shelf was empty of each yield

Besides being a wonderful record and resource in that way, these Harvest Notes also become a very special treasure from year to year. They're preserving our family's history in a special way—a record of the day-to-day homemaking tasks that are so important in our lives. I dare say that stumbling upon such notes from my parents or grandparents would be a true treasure.

Make

....

Soule-Sa Salsa

My family looks forward to the coming of tomato harvest season all year long. Between what we grow on our own, what we get from our community farm and farmer's market, and whatever else we can scrounge up along the way, it's one food we preserve more than any others. Lasting all year long in pizza sauce and pasta sauce and . . . Salsa! Or rather, as my babes coined it several years back, "Soule-Sa!" Here is our recipe for the tastiest salsa we know and love.

WHAT YOU'LL NEED

5 cups tomatoes, peeled and diced
1 cup red onion, diced
1 habanero pepper (or other pepper of your liking), seeded and minced
4 cloves garlic, minced
2 jalapeño peppers, seeded and minced
1 teaspoon black pepper
1 teaspoon cumin
2 tablespoons salt
1/8 cup honey

⅛ cup lemon juice

¼ cup cilantro, minced

6 ounces tomato paste

15 ounces tomato sauce (or 2 cups if using your own homemade sauce)

WHAT TO DO

Add all ingredients to a large stockpot. Bring the mixture to
a boil and maintain it for 15 minutes. Eat, freeze, or can as
desired.

Note: Be sure to adjust the ratios as needed for the appropriate canning method you are using. I recommend the
book *Putting Food By* for that information.

Do

························

Have a Preserving Party

There is magic to be found in a kitchen busy with the activity of preserving a season's harvest. I find great joy in both the busy activity of doing so with my little ones, and also the quiet solitude in the moments I am alone preserving. Working with our hands in this way, with the harvest of right now, feels so wonderful.

But there is another way to work on such canning and preserving—one that has been done for centuries before us by women throughout the world. Preserving with friends—or a "home canning party" as my grandmother always called it. Spending a day in the kitchen with friends laughing, talking, dreaming, sharing stories, and cooking together is pure bliss! Everyone will leave feeling full of each other and full of the harvest which they can share with their own families. There are many ways you can organize a Preserving Party, catered to the harvest, homes, and friends you wish to involve. I've gathered a few suggestions below.

1. Seek the knowledge! If no one among you is an experienced canner, be sure to follow the guidelines found online or in resource books (see the sidebar on page 177) in relation to your tools, preparation, and recipes, as well as preserving methods and instructions. But better than a book (or alongside), might there be an older woman in your community who would love to share this knowledge with you? Invite her to your party!

2. Gather your materials. Plan with your friends who should bring what equipment. It might be helpful to have one person gather all the ingredients and materials while sharing the financial cost evenly with everyone participating. You will need food to harvest; glass jars, rings, and lids; a canner (depending on your method of preserving); jar lifters; and recipe ingredients.

3. Have fun! Bring snacks, music, wine, aprons, and a good sense of humor! Don't rush it, but plan on a good, full, long day of preserving for everyone.

4. If the summer season feels too busy for you and your friends to gather in this way, why not pop your fruit—or whatever the harvest may be—in bags in the freezer? When the quiet of midwinter hits, a little jam making session with friends might be just the right thing for warmth.

SOULE FAMILY FAVORITE PRESERVING BOOKS

Ball Complete Book of Home Preserving by Judy Kingry and Lauren Devine

The Backyard Homestead by Carleen Madigan

Putting Food By by Janet Greene, Ruth Hertzberg, and Beatrice Vaughan

October

Embracing the Dark

There's a precious darkness found in the days of autumn. Literally, our days are darker as we move closer toward the shortest day of the year. Leading up to the Solstice, each day, minute by minute, gets just a little bit shorter, just a little bit cooler, and just a little bit less sun. Darkness begins to encircle us.

If I close my eyes on any October day, I can smell this rich darkness we call autumn. Our senses are alert and awake with the scents of woodpiles chopped or burning in the woodstove, apples sliced or in sauce, and fresh herbs drying for the winter seasons to come. Not to mention the earthy, musty smell of fall "dirt"—the wet, cold ground upon which the bright, crunchy leaves are falling. All these smells together, stirred and swirled, are reminiscent of a fall soup left on a stove all afternoon long. Full of the sustenance of now, in preparation of the season ahead. Our hands are busy with the labor of the season, preparing for what is to come. We chop wood and hope that there is enough to last the winter through. We put our harvest by and fill the pantry shelves as full as we can. All of it done with the acute and very real awareness of what is to come—the darker, colder, days of winter ahead.

Surely the way we prepare for the season to come varies greatly from the ancestors of our past or, for that matter, from people around the globe. For our ancesters, autumn preparations were not a conscious political, environmental, and spiritual choice, necessarily . . . but rather a necessity of life. A necessity that meant the difference between a full winter's belly or being hungry. The difference between warmth and cold. The difference between—sometimes—life and death.

I think about this as I spend my days in the kitchen preparing food, or cutting more kindling, or tightening up the windows for the winter's breeze that could blow right through. I am grateful that for us, this is a choice. This is how we have chosen to live, and we do so knowing full well that we are able to turn on the oil heat we have as backup if the wood runs out in March. That a grocery store is no less than a mile away from our home, full of everything we could need. This is all true, and I rely upon that knowledge. But my heart remains with the weight of the season's work. I embrace it as an opportunity to be here and now, present and yet planning mindfully and thoughtfully for the future ahead of me. I embrace it as an opportunity to move slowly and enjoy the beauty in the darkness. I embrace it as an important lesson for my children in both the joys, sorrows, peaks, and valleys of our lives—of our seasonal year.

This darkness is not something we often have a chance to reflect upon in our culture. There is little opportunity for it, as a solution to our seasonal needs is almost always nearby—and used without thought. But oh, this time of year—the slowness, the darkness, the death around us in the natural world—is full of its own kind of beauty.

I want my children to understand this, to know this kind of natural danger. The kind of danger that has them fully aware of the harsh realities of this earth, and yet still open to embracing, discovering, and exploring it all with respect and curiosity. It wasn't that long ago in our culture's past in which children's days had a bit more danger. We rode bikes without helmets. We played well after dark with our friends. We went into the woods, alone. I don't suggest we abandon bike helmets or keep our children unaware of their personal safety—quite the opposite. I seek to find the balance between keeping them safe and allowing them the freedom to explore and embrace danger in their own beautiful ways. To hand them common sense alongside a pocketknife when they have the knowledge, respect, and curiosity to use one. To embrace adventure on their own in the woods. To explore and discover the wilderness at nighttime. To embrace the beauty in the darkness.

This is what I learn in the autumn months.

PAPA

Common Ground

Under a crisp bluebird sky the breeze blows tinges of cool to mingle and swirl through the warm rays of the sun. We've journeyed together, as a complete family, to meet with friends and strangers alike in celebration of harvest and life at the Common Ground Country Fair.

The children call out their pick of things they simply cannot miss before the day is complete. Calvin likes the sheepdogs but really he wants to spend hours doing summersaults into the hay pile and roughhousing with the other kids his age. Ezra waxes poetic over what he'd like to get for lunch and then wants a ride on the horse-pulled wagon, and, oh, also to have his face painted. Maybe his face painted first and then a wagon ride, but he really wants French fries . . . and apple cider. Adelaide plays the same game with all of the animals she plans to visit, starting with chickens and working her way up to the sheep and goats and cows and horses. And of course, she doesn't want to miss the kids' vegetable parade either.

Amanda and I look at each other and realize that our list of Mama and Papa activities will be short again this year, but the kids won't be this little forever. We walk slowly, Harper enjoying his lofty seat atop the back of his Mama. I wonder what those wide eyes are taking in as we step into a symphony of activity and the day begins.

Amid a myriad of people busy at tasks of the hand, our feet carry us through the crowd and past the spinners at the fiber tent. Amanda ducks in for a few skeins of gorgeous organic yarn to support the locals and her habit, a treat for her each year.

We go through the rabbit tent and then the chickens as Ada rambles on in a stream of consciousness about the variations in each particular animal. Nobody has more fun at the fair than she does. I stop with the boys to watch a man shear wool from sheep, his hands working, efficient and quick, as he speaks to the onlookers about his process. I remind Ezra of the sweater he is wearing which his Mama made, of the spinners, and of the yarn we just got.

"It's like *Pelle's New Suit*," he says, about a children's book we've read over the years.

"Just like that," I say.

He watches the man work and adds, "It's like *everything*."

We laugh as the sheepshearer gets caught up in conversation, leaving his half-sheared sheep to wait, patiently, for his return.

Beginning to feel the vibe now, we stroll past some of the food vendors and get excited about the lunchtime to come as delicious wafts float by in olfactory delight. Nearing the stables where the larger animals are kept, en route to quell Ezra's disappointment that we didn't get to eat lunch at 10 a.m., we climb aboard the horse-drawn wagon for a ride around the grounds, $1 apiece.

As we get ready to roll, I watch an old Maine farmer holding court, a deeply tanned face under his baseball hat, flannel shirt tucked over his belly into blue jeans. He's talking to a young couple with tattooed skin under their overalls, windblown long hair. They listen intently to the knowledge he is passing along and question him intelligently for specifics. His accent, a thick Maine trademark, makes me feel at home. I watch this interaction of ideas and see that it symbolizes, for me, what I am most excited about today. Connection. To our food, to our resources, to our history, to our future, to each other.

We pass a group of drummers adding a layer to the senses, and I close my eyes to the warm sun as we pass, the click of the horses' hooves in front of the wagon steady and surprisingly light under such a weight.

The day wears on amidst the normal trials of a family at the fair. Tired and hungry children getting rested and fed among a sea of other families doing the same. We negotiate the needs and hopes of each and take in as much as our minds will permit. We see old friends and share stories and hugs and remark at how things change. We listen to experts of the elements speak on capturing energy from the sun, building arches out of stone, spinning mills to harness the power of the wind, and protecting our watersheds. We listen to music. We dance.

It all boils together as we walk over the land. Political action, sustainable living, natural birth, organic farming . . . inspirations and passions being shared.

We lie in the grass and regroup and share our thoughts from the day and let the kids pick one more thing they would like to do before its end. Harper crawls excitedly across the yard, happy to be out of his pack again. As the sun drops into twilight we begin the long meander off the grounds. We walk past vendors, busy tidying after a long day of celebration, and past animals at rest in their beds of hay, worn out from the work of being on display.

The evening air cools rapidly, and from a small hill I look over the fair, nestled against the edge of the forest, surrounded by leaves alight with colors of the harvest. Peaceful. We walk on and soak in the feeling. We pass the drummers in the same place as earlier, still kicking out their beat. The hands have changed as the musicians grew tired and left the circle, but the beat carries on into the encroaching darkness. The beat goes on.

I watch Calvin and Ezra and realize that this is more than tradition for them; it is normal. Part of their year and their everyday chorus. I watch Adelaide talking sweetly with Harper, asking if he had fun at the fair. I am filled with hope and pride at a world that is so capable. So kindhearted. We are leaving, but we are full.

Make

....

Nature Stamps

Stamping with bits of the outside world is a wonderful way to enjoy nature in a new way. To discover some new plants in your travels, perhaps, and to carry that exploration into the art of your inside play. From a walk in the country or city park to the process of making prints, the entire family can participate in the process of crafting together. This project comes from artist, mama, and nature lover Maya Donenfeld of Maya*Made.

Nature Stamps by Maya Donenfeld

Experimenting with different stamping items is the fun part of this project. Some of my favorite materials include poppy pods right after the petals have fallen off (although dry ones can be revived with a soak in warm water), any flowers in the preblossoming stage (campanula work very well), walnut halves, and lotus pods. Seek out any other bits of nature that have a firm and interesting surface.

WHAT YOU'LL NEED

Bits of nature for stamping (see suggestions above)
Well-inked stamp pads (I like Color Box and Versa Craft)
Various paper and cardstock for stamping on (paper bags and
cereal boxes turned inside out are good recycled options)
Batting or old towel
Scissors or a paper cutter
Glue stick

WHAT TO DO

1. Take a walk and gather bits of interesting stamping materials from nature. Collect a variety so you can see how different objects respond to the ink. If you have hard pieces of nature, such as walnuts, pods, and so on, they might print best after spending some time soaking in warm water to soften them up a bit.

2. Prepare your work area by spreading a protective covering over your work surface. Lay out a small towel or piece of cotton batting. Place some of your papers on the towel and some directly on your work surface to create different effects.

3. Experiment stamping on firm and soft surfaces with each object. See which impressions you prefer.

4. After your prints are dry, cut out small sections and adhere them to cards for handmade stationery. Try making a bookmark by pasting printed paper to cardstock (or a cereal box). Attach some twine to a nature keepsake,

such as an acorn or a shell, and thread the twine through a hole punched in the paper. Use prints as gift tags, wrapping paper, or note cards. The possibilities are endless!

Make

·····················

A String of Leaves

Have you ever looked closely at the leaves around you? Really and truly looked at them? The diversity within each and every leaf—from tree to tree and branch to branch—is astounding. The shapes are complicated and complex, the lines many and varied. Identifying the trees around us by their leaves is great fun. It's a joy to truly know the trees you live amidst.

This project was born on a day like any other at home. Walking around our modest suburban backyard, Ezra noticed a bright yellow leaf he apparently had never seen before. He thought it was beautiful. (It was!) We began comparing it to the others around it, and to those on the neighboring trees and bushes and shrubs. His brother and sister joined in on the action, and soon the entire family was gathering leaves from every corner of our home—each on a mission to find a different kind than had been found already. Soon, we had a rather large pile of leaves gathered in front of us, which we brought inside for further examination. A little while later, we came up with this idea of a banner of *our* leaves—an artistic, visual reminder of the many trees and leaves that surround our very home.

This project could certainly be expanded to include all sorts of the nature bits that you find around your home. It needn't be limited to trees and leaves. But the concept of having it be things from your "outside home" is a special one—making the inside and outside of our homes—our days, our lives, and spirits—just a bit more connected and together.

CRAFTING NOTES

Soft-Kut is a rubber block, roughly 1/2" thick. I prefer block printing with this material because it's easy to cut into any size and also a bit easier to work than a traditional woodblock, thereby making it accessible to younger crafters. Still, safety precautions should be used with young children, particularly when using the lino cutters. Depending on age and ability, that particular step might be best for adults and older children.

WHAT YOU'LL NEED

Soft-Kut printing blocks
Water-based block printing ink
Brayer
Lino cutters and handle
Newspaper for surface
Pencil for drawing
Sheet of glass, metal, cardboard, or a palette for spreading
   ink (I use a cut piece of glass with duct tape on all edges to
   keep fingers safe)
Linen or cotton fabric pieces at a size larger than your stamp
Twine
Clothespins or a sewing machine
Scissors or an X-Acto knife for cutting the block

WHAT TO DO

1. Most importantly, gather leaves! Have yourself a lovely walk, a stroll around your yard, a park, a trail—wherever you go most! Choose leaves that are appealing to you and

different from one another. Study them, play with them, inspect them (use a magnifying glass!). If you'd like, use a tree identification book to find out what each is. And then, gather them up and bring them to your work area.

2. If you're working in a space that needs to be protected, lay newspaper or a vinyl cloth on your work surface. Cut the linen to your desired size (my stamps are all roughly 3" x 5", so my fabric squares started at 5" x 7"). Cut out as many pieces as you would like. Lay them flat and spread them out, ready for stamping.

3. Cut the rubber to your desired stamp size using scissors or an X-Acto knife. Especially for young children, you want the stamp to be manageable in size so they have the time and patience to finish designing and carving it, but also not so small that the detail is too difficult to work. I generally cut mine to 3" x 5". Using a pencil, draw your leaf (by tracing or observing and drawing) directly onto the rubber.

4. Using the appropriate lino cutter (for larger areas to cut, use the largest-size cutter, and for more fine detail, use the smaller-size cutter), begin to cut away the outline of your leaf. Be sure to cut away from you for proper impact as well as safety! Remember that what you cut away will be "blank," and not covered in ink. The parts and pieces left behind are what will have ink and add color to your fabric.

5. Continue cutting the shape as desired. It needn't be precise—the very nature of lino cutting involves carving lines, and having those visible is okay! It's part of the process and part of the finished piece as well! When you are satisfied with the cutting, trim the edges of the rubber as needed.

6. Squeeze a bit of ink (about the size of a quarter to start) onto your palette. Roll the brayer back and forth over the ink with even pressure until it is covered. Set your stamp on a flat surface, design side up. Using the brayer, roll the ink over the top of the stamp, coating your design evenly in ink.

7. Carefully pick the stamp up, turning it over in your hands, and press it down on the center of your fabric square. Remove the stamp, and repeat these steps as often as desired with your other stamps and fabric squares!

8. Allow the fabric to dry while you clean up the work area— and for as long as the ink manufacturer's instructions state (generally a few hours is enough time). The brayer can be washed with regular dishwashing soap and warm water.

9. When the ink is dry, attach the fabric squares to a length of twine. Clothespins are a lovely way to hang your squares if you'd rather not sew. Hand stitching is also a great option, as well as machine stitching. Simply fold over the top edge and sew it in place, being sure to leave space to later insert the twine. This banner is intended to be a bit rustic and natural in its finished state, so don't worry about getting precise or detailed stitching.

10. Hang your String of Leaves in a special spot inside your house (or even outside!) and enjoy the wonder of the leaves that truly are all around you.

Da

....

Take a Seasons Walk

A favorite tradition in our home is to take a First Day walk: A walk on the first day of the season, whichever one it may be. A walk on which we search for the season. Walks are a regular part of our days, but this First Day walk is something special, as the intention of truly noticing and paying attention is present in each step that we take. On this walk, we notice and talk about both the subtle and dynamic shifts that the earth is displaying around us. On this special mission of a walk, the focus of everyone from young to old becomes one of discovery. Who will be the first to find signs of spring? What will those signs be?

In our family, this walk often happens on the same trail near our home. While it can be done anywhere, there's an extra special element added to the noticing when you are in the same location but with the changed season for a landscape. We see and notice on each of our First Day walks the progression of a tree's leaves from bud, to green, to red, to bare. We see and notice the way the insects are present and then not, the way the small woodland animals move differently than they did during our last walk of the season before. It's the perfect walk upon which to bring a magnifying glass and get just a little bit closer to the earth.

As parents, we often find ourselves noticing the ways in which the children have changed, too, on these little walks of ours. The sandals they wear in summer give way to sneakers, snow boots, and then mud boots. The feet, bodies, voices, and minds of the little ones inside those clothes and on the trail have grown and changed, too. Such as the earth they are noticing around them has also changed.

In the busy days of family life, where so often the days can fly right on by, First Day walks are one easy, simple, and lovely way to slow things down just a little bit. The tradition becomes a simple and beautiful way to mark the changing seasons, the passage of time, and the growth of a family.

November

Crafting the Life

It is in the late months of the year that I feel our pace picking up. The rush to prepare for the season ahead of us is on, combined with a flurry of holiday activity and festivities, not to mention all the crafting and making I would like to do for the gift-giving season in front of us. Our days become full—full of richness and wonderful moments, but full nonetheless. It's in these months that I find it most essential to stay clear and focused on the life that I want to live. I find myself thinking daily, sometimes hourly, about the ways I need to direct my actions to incorporate the important pieces of creativity, nature, and family that we value into our busy lives.

My little one, Ezra, made me a Mother's Day comic book a few years ago called "Mama of Knit Knit." Mama of Knit Knit is a supermama superhero with amazing powers. She can fly, she can make herself and those around her invisible, and most importantly, that Mama can knit her way out of any jam. Stuck at the top of a crumbling building? Mama of Knit Knit can knit a cape to fly! But alas, that supermama is indeed just a myth. The truth of course is that sometimes our homes are messy, sometimes we eat popcorn for dinner, sometimes there is fighting, and sometimes we parents wonder just how it is that we're going to get through a day. None of us can do it all. Letting ourselves believe that—that someone else has it so much more together than we do—is just a distraction and takes us away from honoring the real work that each of us is doing in our everyday lives or the real work that we could be doing.

The reality is that none of us are superheroes, and that incorporating creativity, slow and mindful living, and seasonal celebration into our daily lives takes practice. The most important piece in crafting the life I want has been choosing carefully what I say yes to. We must say yes to the chances that excite us, yes to the things that bring us closer to our family, the earth, and each other. Yes to art and nature walks and reading stories. Yes to the important things—whatever we deem those to be.

On the flip side of that is recognizing the importance of saying no to those things that do not bring us closer to the kind of life we want to be living. The specifics of what that might be certainly vary from person to person. For some it might mean letting go of the television, for some it might mean saying goodbye to just one more committee we are on or resisting those new pair of shoes. But the important thing is that we are questioning and evaluating the choices we make in our daily life. The choices that either do or do not allow us room for the kind of connection, growth, and exploration that we want for ourselves and our families.

I'm reminded too, this time of year, of the importance of like-minded community in our efforts to live the life we want. Having friends upon whom we can call for company, advice, opinions, or laughter is essential in our striving toward the life we love. Whether it be a gathering of friends for a Preserving Party or a community food event, or an online connection with someone thousands of miles away living with similar values, these connections are so helpful to our journey.

With these things in mind, we move forward in our days of work and play. We move forward with mindful, intentional baby steps on a path we've chosen, making time for the things that are important to us in our days, making plans for the things we wish for ourselves in the future, and sharing it all the way with those we love.

PAPA

Thank You

It's late now, and the cold gray days settle heavily into our bones as the weight of impending darkness pushes down a willing and tired sun, draped in clouds. The sharp autumn winds remain to shake the last leaves free from the slipping grip of their trees. Temperatures stick toward freezing as a light rain falls steadily to dampen ground and spirits alike. The earth dies every November, hosting a funeral march for miracles that rose gracefully out of the early spring rains and shimmered prominently in the warm breeze of July amidst a sea of admiring smiles. The fireworks of a vibrant autumn bring the dance to its end, and we file out of the theatre in bittersweet procession, grateful to be witness to such a show. The curtain closes, and we are left standing in a field of matted grass surrounded by the stark forest, black, imposing, and raw.

Days move with a solemn slowness at this time in the North. We struggle but manage to fasten boots and loosen limbs to prepare ourselves for the work ahead. Raking against ground, clearing a space for the encroaching snows to settle. Swinging axes in an arc to reduce trees to tidy piles. Stashing away the last of the year's harvest. Providing shelter and comfort against a winter that drops without warning, in an instant.

Our eyes adjust slowly to the shift in light. Fueled by hard days of work, hearts beat on and, eventually, focus returns. A neighbor emerges with an extended hand to shake and lend in task. As the casualties of a season lay to rot, we carry on and embrace our survival.

Great feasts are readied while the excitement of children swirls through a house. Bodies in familiar motion come together and harmonize in celebration. Families travel across great expanse to join with loved ones and to gather around a table in joy. Conversations fill the rooms, as histories are told and new stories made. The elderly sit comfortably and wise and smile knowingly, with gracious love. They have lived through these generations and remember how their legs, as youngsters, churned around and about their grandparents' home. Hundreds of seasons passing before their eyes, giving faith that the next was sure to follow. Bearing witness to the speed with which the earth circles the sun, they see clearly that these kids will soon be seated and counted as the old at all occasions, holding the weight of those that pass before and learning that all of their time together is only now. No amount of worry or regret will amount to changing the demise that is found in each cycle of life. So, it is natural that the elders smile and remember and remind the young.

Tales of struggle and family, adventure and love, recount harder days and lend gentle hints to be aware of how we came to be here: Spinning yarns of great fish in abundance strung on a line and feeding a crew of woodsmen that work dawn until dusk. Sleeping in bunkhouses and dreaming in unison of the loved ones they support from afar. Rising to the same chores with vigor and appreciation to have such accommodations and luck. Caring for old farms and houses with little heat and many needs to which siblings were required to tend before and after long walks to school. Rising above grief to hold moments of happiness and allowing those moments to feed their soul and bring reason to their efforts. Communities of immigrants in a new world, strong and brave and full of hope, putting their very selves into the land.

Sitting, with attention rapt, we listen in admiration to the quiet words of our older family members and wonder, what is the story of our life? We hold each other hand in hand, young and old, and look from eye to eye. Where we stand is the story of our days. Each hand a chapter, each life a book, each heart alive. United, we sit to eat and offer a simple thanks for all that it is we have. We understand. Thank You.

Make

....

Nature's Paper

It was a wasps' nest embedded in the walls of our house that led our family on a paper making adventure. When the hive was removed, we all inspected and marveled in fascination. We learned that wasps build their paper hives by gathering bits of fibers and weeds, chewing them into a paste, and spitting it out to create the walls of their hive.

Making your own paper is incredibly fun and perfect for so many ages (what toddler doesn't love ripping up bits of paper?). Experiment with adding bits of nature into your paper—dried leaves, grass, and straw will make for interesting smells, textures, and a natural-looking paper that any little one would be proud of.

WHAT YOU'LL NEED

Paper scraps—computer paper, printer paper, newspaper (which will make a grayish paper), magazines, toilet paper, watercolor paper or cardstock, tissue paper, napkins, and so on

Nature bits—dried leaves, grass, straw, stems, flowers, and more

Sponge

Brayer, if available

Blender

Cookie sheet

Baking rack

Mesh window screening

A piece of flannel or cotton fabric (slightly larger than your wood frame)

Wool or flannel fabric for drying on

Basin (a roasting pan is ideal)

Wood for frame (a wooden picture frame could be used)

Nails and hammer, or staples and stapler (for building the frame)

WHAT TO DO

1. Tear the paper pieces into 2" squares. If you are using cardstock and heavier papers, allow them to soak in a bowl of water for several hours to soften.

2. To make your frame, either gather a premade picture frame or attach pieces of wood with nails or staples to make your own. Cut a piece of mesh window screening slightly larger than your wood frame. Staple the screen to the sides of the frame, keeping the screen as taut as possible.

3. Fill a basin (a roasting pan works well) with a few inches of water. Place your wood frame in the water, screen side down (it will float). Next to your basin, set up the cookie sheet with a baking rack on top; next to that, lay out your sheet of wool or flannel that will serve as a drying area.

4. Place the pieces of paper in a blender, and fill it 3/4 of the way with water. And any nature bits you'd like. Blend until smooth. Your paper pulp should be liquid, not as clumpy as oatmeal. If it's clumpy, add more water.

5. To start making your paper, pour a bit of pulp from the blender into the wood frame (which is floating and half immersed in the tub of water). Fill it to the surface of the water. Swish the frame in the water (without submerging it) to even out the pulp. Slowly lift the entire frame above the water, allowing the water to fall below into the basin.

6. Place the frame on your baking rack on top of the cookie sheet. Using a sponge, carefully press the pulp against the screen to drain the water. Don't worry if the pulp begins to lift, it is forgiving at this point and can easily be put back in place with your fingers. (If you want to include whole

flower petals or other such intact pieces of nature, work them into the pulpy paper now.)

7. Place your clean sheet of fabric on top of the pulpy paper. Press evenly, squeezing out more water. If you have a brayer available, use it to squeeze out more water; if not, gentle fingers work!

8. Keeping the fabric pressed firmly against the paper, carefully flip the frame upside down, so that the fabric is underneath. Scratch the backside of the mesh screening to transfer the paper from the mesh and frame to the fabric entirely.

9. Bring this piece of fabric gently to the wool/flannel drying area. Flip it once again so that the pulp is against the drying fabric. Carefully remove the transfer fabric by rolling it away from the paper.

10. Allow your paper to dry.

Make

....

Everyday Oat Bread

This bread, heavy on the honey and oats, is much loved in the cooler months at my home. With a bit of everyone's favorite spread handy— nut butters, jams, and butter—a loaf can make a perfect anytime-of-day snack, or even lunch! It toasts well, it's fairly quick to make, and it's easy for little hands to help make—hence, the "any day, everyday" nature of it. Around our house we call this WHO bread for wheat, honey, and oats. If you prefer bread machines (sometimes we do—especially my little ones who can do it all by themselves), there's a similar recipe for you too!

WHAT YOU'LL NEED

2 cups warm water

4¹/₂ teaspoons active dry yeast (2 packages)

4 tablespoons honey

2 tablespoons brown sugar

5 cups flour (plus an additional 1 cup for kneading)

1 cup rolled oats

2 teaspoons salt

4 tablespoons butter, at room temperature

Olive or canola oil, for the bowl and bread pan

WHAT TO DO

Pour the warm water into a small bowl. Mix in the yeast,
honey, and brown sugar. Whisk until everything is
combined and the mixture begins to get frothy. Set it
aside to proof for 10 minutes or until foamy.

In a separate large bowl, mix the flour, salt, oats, and
butter. Mix until the butter is worked through. (Using
your hands—and your little ones' hands—works best!
Alternatively, a food processor or stand mixer can do this
for you.)

Pour the yeast mixture into the flour mixture. Mix until thoroughly combined. If it's too sticky, add just a bit more flour.

Pour the dough out onto kneading surface. Knead for 10 minutes or so, adding up to 1 cup of flour as needed to prevent sticking. Stop kneading when the dough begins to be elastic.

Place the dough in a lightly oiled bowl. Cover it with a damp cloth, and let rise in a warm place for 1 hour. Punch down the dough gently, and let it rise for another half an hour.

Turn the dough out onto a floured surface. Divide it into 2 balls for 2 loaves. Gently knead each ball for 2 to 3 minutes. Place the dough balls into lightly oiled bread pans. Press the top of the dough with the back of your hands to flatten and evenly shape the dough in the pan. Sprinkle the top of the dough with a bit of oats. Cover again, and let the dough sit in a warm place for a half an hour to rise 1 more time.

Preheat the oven to 350°F. Bake the bread for 40 minutes, or until the top begins to appear golden.

Let cool in the pan for 10 minutes. Remove from pan to fully cool on a wire rack.

A Bread Machine Alternative

Please note that all bread machines act a little differently, so you may need to experiment and adjust this recipe according to yours.

WHAT YOU'LL NEED

1¼ cups water
2 tablespoons honey

2 teaspoons butter, at room temperature

1 teaspoon salt

3 cups flour (we do 2 cups unbleached white, 1 cup whole wheat pastry)

$1/2$ cup rolled oats

1 tablespoon brown sugar

1 teaspoon cinnamon

$2^1/4$ teaspoons active dry yeast (1 package)

WHAT TO DO

Insert ingredients into your machine in the order listed above. Set your machine to basic with a medium crust. Makes a $1^1/2$ lb. loaf.

Do

....

Use Natural Dyes

Dyeing fabric and fiber with materials found in the natural world is a family favorite and a wonderful project for all ages. There are endless possibilities for color when we use the earth's palette as our guide. We're often surprised by what color a certain material yields when added to fabric—quite often it is so different from the original source. That's part of the fun, so keep an open mind about your end results, and experiment with whatever you have available in your own backyard!

NATURAL MATERIALS FOR DYEING

Red—dandelion root, beets, rose hips, chokecherries, blackberries, hibiscus

Orange—sassafras, onion skin, carrot root, turmeric, pomegranate

Yellow—marigold, burdock, celery leaves, tea, dandelions, sunflowers

Green—spinach leaves, nettle, red onion, yarrow, foxglove, sorrel

Blue/purple—mulberries, red cabbage, hyacinth, maple tree bark

Brown—oat bark, juniper berries, tea bags, birch bark, walnut hulls

CRAFTING NOTES

If you are dyeing yarn, open it up into a large circle while keeping it wound in its skein. Tie it loosely at several points to hold it in its skein while going through the dye process.

These instructions will work well for things that aren't washed often—play silks, scarves, yarn for knitting, and other playthings. If you are hoping for the color to stay through many washes, consider using synthrapol as a prewash, as well as a postwash to help set the fabric a little more thoroughly.

The photographed projects are dyed with turmeric and tea bags.

WHAT YOU'LL NEED

Vegetables, plants, or herbs for dyeing material

A large stockpot (I use an extra-large canning pot; 2 pots is ideal)

White vinegar

Blank fabric or undyed fiber (cotton, wool, and silk will work best; polyester is trickier to dye)

Mesh strainer

WHAT TO DO

1. Fill a large pot with water and heat until boiling. Add 3 cups of white vinegar. Add your fabric or yarn to the pot (the fabric should be able to move freely in the pot—you may need to save the rest for another batch). Remove the pot from the heat. Let the pot sit until it reaches room temperature. Remove the fabric/yarn and wring it lightly to remove some water. Dispose of the vinegar solution.

2. Prepare your dye bath by once again filling the pot with water. Add your dye materials, and stir well. Heat to boiling, and maintain a boil for 30 minutes or so. Use the mesh strainer to remove the vegetable/plant bits that are in the water (if you are using a powdery material, or something contained, like tea bags, they can stay in for richer color).

3. Add the vinegar-soaked fabric/yarn to the pot. Add another 1 cup of vinegar. Lower the heat to a simmer, cover, and stir often. Check the fabric/yarn periodically to check the color and determine when you think it's done. Depending on what you're using and how deep you'd like the color, this can be anywhere from 30 minutes to 1 hour.

4. When the color is saturated to your satisfaction, remove the pot (still covered) from the heat. If you'd still like the color to be a little bit deeper, leave the fabric/yarn in until it comes to room temperature.

5. Remove the fabric/yarn, and rinse it under cold tap water. Hang to dry.

SOULE FAMILY FAVORITE NATURAL DYEING BOOKS

The Complete Guide to Natural Dyeing: Fabric, Yarn, and Fiber by Eva Lambert and Tracy Kendall

The Handbook of Natural Plant Dyes by Sasha Duerr

Natural Dyes and Home Dyeing by Rita Adrosko

Wild Color: The Complete Guide to Making and Using Natural Dyes by Jenny Dean

Da

....

Encourage Meditation

In the autumnal season, it's natural that we find ourselves turning inward for reflection and comfort before the chaos of the season. This trend is particularly true for children, who are less in control of the activities and events around them. Yoga and meditation are wonderful opportunities for children to find a bit of that inner peace in times of need, allowing them to connect to themselves and their voices in this seasonal time of shifting. I've asked my friend Heather Fontenot to share some of the ways she helps her children (and herself) find peace and comfort through meditation and yoga.

Using short meditations, either upon waking, before sleep, or during activities such as hiking and exploration, children can connect to this shift in seasons. Guided meditation can be used with almost any age group of children, but for the wee ones it should be no longer than five minutes. Allow your child a chance to reflect on each part of the meditation, and provide moments of complete silence that ground your child to the present moment.

Meditation for Children by Heather Fontenot
SEATED OR LYING MEDITATION

Have your child either sit in a crisscross-applesauce position or lie comfortably on the floor. Allow him to spend about one minute quietly coming into his own, and encourage your child to relax fully.

When he's ready, guide your child as follows:

Bring your hands to your stomach, and take a few normal breaths. Draw your awareness into your tummy, and feel the breath flowing and moving with each inhale and exhale.

As the earth moves inward for the coming winter, how will you do the same? Visualize the trees and the grass and the leaves all shedding a layer of themselves, getting ready for new growth. What can you shed or leave behind that allows for new growth come spring?

Bring your awareness back to the present moment, take a big inhalation, and exhale fully.

WALKING MEDITATION

This is a special meditation that an older child can do on her own, or that a younger child could do with your guidance.

Find a special place to take a quiet walk. Standing still for just a moment, look around you and observe the earth as it is slowly preparing to turn inward for the winter ahead. What do you notice about the colors around you? How does the air feel against your skin?

Begin walking at a normal pace. Notice the sounds around you. As your walk continues, come to an awareness of your breath and take a nice, deep inhalation. As you exhale, release your breath all the way down into the earth. Continue walking this way, feeling the connection that you have with the earth below.

CANDLE MEDITATION

In a quiet and dark room, light a single candle. Ask your child to quietly gaze into the candle while breathing deeply. Allow him to sit this way for at least a few minutes. Before blowing the candle out, remind your child that the earth is heading into a darker phase as we move toward the shortest day of the year. Ask your child to set an intention for something that he would like to face, conquer, or overcome in the day ahead.

LISTENING MEDITATION

Ask your child to join you outside on a blanket or chair. Have her close her eyes and take a few deep breaths. Allow her to listen intently to all of the sounds of the seasons. After one to two minutes, ask her to share with you what she heard, and how the earth is preparing for the season ahead.

Yoga for Children by Heather Fontenot
EXPLORING THE BREATH

Have your child lay flat on a hard surface, with a thin mat or towel underneath. When he is settled, guide your child as follows:

Stretch out on your back, relaxing your arms and legs fully. Breathe normally for a few moments. Allow yourself to take a full, deep inhalation, and let it out with a big sigh. Take a few more breaths just like this one. Draw your breath into each of your toes, and as you exhale, release your toes fully to the floor. Now breathe deeply into your legs,

and as you exhale, relax them deeply into the floor. (Have your child repeat this with his pelvis, tummy, chest, fingers, arms, shoulders, neck, and head.) Now take the biggest breath that you can possibly take, and then release your entire body fully into the earth. Lay quietly for a few extra moments, and when you are ready, gently sit up.

Encouraging children to take long, deep breathes and to release the air completely. These actions promote relaxation and a genuine connection to their ability to relax, calm, and root themselves fully.

Every season brings a time for transitions, and the shift between autumn and winter can provide children with an opportunity for deep personal growth and a stronger sense of self. The earlier little ones begin to recognize their own cycles of life as matching those of the earth they inhabit, the better their sense of place in this world will be.

SOULE FAMILY FAVORITE KIDS YOGA AND MEDITATION BOOKS

Each Breath a Smile by Sister Thue Nghiem and Thich Nhat Hahn
My Daddy Is a Pretzel: Yoga for Parents and Kids by Baron Baptiste
Peaceful Piggy Meditation by Kerry Lee Maclean
Starbright—Meditations for Children by Maureen Garth

December

The Work of Home

It's quiet this time of year. The trees are bare, the leaves have gone. The critters we are so used to seeing outside our windows are settled down for a while, done with their busy autumn season of preparing and storing for winter's months. The garden beds are covered and at rest, and everything outside has changed slowly from bright reds and oranges to a subtle shift of browns and grays that will be around until the white begins to fall. It seems as though the living in the woods and out of doors have gone underground now. It's calmer, quieter out there.

With that shift in energy comes the presence of an inward energy in our home. For the months ahead, the inside walls of our home will be our primary setting day in and day out. Making that home, and making it just right for us, is a role I treasure dearly. I love placing my energy here this very time of year.

It's so very easy in our busy days and busy lives, and particularly at this busy time of year, to feel overwhelmed by our tasks at home. Life with four children, with so much making and doing ourselves, can be chaotic and full of life's messes. The laundry that piles up, the dishes that need washing, and more and more meals to prepare than one thinks could be possible for one family. The possibility of being flustered and overwhelmed by all that lies ahead for tasks is ever present and can lead quickly to days full of not enjoying the work of home.

But I do believe—if it is your passion and of your choosing—that there is such peace and contentment to be found in creating a nurturing, nourishing home for our families. The secret to that peace and contentment lies in being mindful of our days and valuing the work that we do at home. The answer lies in simply slowing down.

Slowing down through our household tasks and responsibilities gives us the opportunity to mindfully create a home for those we love. It allows us to reflect on our lives with thought and care. It creates a comfortable daily rhythm in our home, making the space, our families, and ourselves comfortable.

Moving slowly through the work of our days means that sometimes the work does not get gone. There are some days that are just too full of play, or activity, or other needs that must be met. Letting go of others' expectations, and sometimes our own expectations of ourselves, is a wonderful blessing. That's what home is after all, a place that allows the room and freedom for us to do as we need and love.

Moving slowly through the work of our days means that we are present in the moments we are in. We are not rushing to get to the next task, but rather fully aware and involved in the act of right now—whatever that may be. Household tasks aren't necessarily events that need to be rushed through or just gotten through. In fact, they are what consume much of our time during our days as a family. To choose to spend them in gratitude and awareness is choosing to bring more peace and contentment into our lives and to share that with our children.

This is the way I strive to live and work, and it's the way I strive for my children to learn about the work of living close to the earth—mindfully, seasonally, and slowly.

Chopping wood for the winter to come, I work methodically and carefully in the interest of my safety and in the interest of doing the job well. I know that I will be grateful in the cold months of February if I have cut the logs to a proper length for our stove or if I have made the stacks neat and strong enough so they will last through the storms to come. In this process of working at the job slowly, I am aware of the leaves falling around me, the smell of the smoke billowing from the nearby wood-stoves, the sound of the late robins in the yard. Sharing this with my children, I see them partake in the same beauty. They notice the things around them as they gather sticks for kindling. The line between their play and their work is blurred as they gather. And most special of all, the conversations we share together in this time—and sometimes, the silence—warm our hearts and will stay with us for all of our lives.

The same can be said of all the seasonal work that we do. Preserving. Preparing. Harvesting. Nurturing the earth. Connecting with each other. They are gifts that living seasonally and simply provides us—a year-round gift from the earth for us to share in if we so choose.

PAPA

Year's End

The first snowflakes float in as a whisper and caress the world gently as a feather. No object is spared as a soft cloak of white is draped across the land. With its arrival, people emerge from their hiding to witness the transformation and feel fresh against the clean slate laid before them. With luck and no small amount of magic, the snow continues to accumulate as beds of soft and icy wonder lay in blankets and widen childish smiles across faces of young and old alike. The light depths of powder serve to cleanse our thoughts and ease worries with their allure.

A storybook of beauty unfolds as children with sleds run laughing to their hills and plow themselves into submersion on repeated attempts. Tired and unstoppable they continue until hunger and the blackness of night force them begrudgingly back inside. Skis, which have been prepped and readied for this day, are strapped on and unleashed with unbridled energy, potential to kinetic. The streets are alive as people continue to appear from hiding and lift their faces to the sky. Shovels appear to clear walkways and steps. Road crews and plow trucks circle, retracing their steps in efficient efforts to clear safe passage for travelers.

The snows continue into the evening and through the night. Bursting through doors to find their footsteps of the previous evening erased from existence, the kids are back out into it with a flurry of limbs and lightness. Crowds gather on the hills nearby and we're brought together in happiness. Quickly, the snow is packed down and sleds are moving fast and far as hands hold bodies to them. Twists and falls in an array of disjointed appendages stretch smiles wide along the slopes. I watch my own taking their turns as natural as the next and find myself shaking my head with wonder at their tiny selves, tucked into puffy warm gear. Their spirit and matter alive on this hillside, celebrating the simple pleasure of snow on the ground.

A miracle of circumstances has brought me here as conscious witness to my own people that I rise with in the morning and lay down with each evening. I could not be more grateful for this moment or this life. On we spin with futures so uncertain as our lives play out and decisions mount and turn off on tangents and bring us always back to right now. These seasons rotate around and through us, and bring us back again, past the fall, and on to the threshold of spring and new and abundant life.

I stand knee-deep in the first snow of the season. I bend to wipe the cold ice off the face of a child. My child. I straighten her mittens and snug down her hat. With a soft kiss on her cheek, I send her back to play.

Make

....

Postcard Block

My son Calvin came up with this clever way to display his favorite post-cards, which he originally displayed in his Winter Wonderland decoration. At the end of the holiday season, we decided the Postcard Block was a wonderful holder for so many treasures one might want to keep on display—artwork, postcards, and even baseball cards. Little ones love working with wood, feeling the texture and weight in their hands. This project is great for the youngest of woodworkers, with just a little bit of help from an adult needed.

WHAT YOU'LL NEED

A fallen branch or log
Sandpaper
A small bow saw (or other handsaw)
Beeswax polish (optional)

WHAT TO DO

1. Gather your desired log from the woods! Look for something approximately 2"–3" in diameter. Any kind of wood will do, choose something that is available and beautiful to

you. Cut the log to your desired size, approximately 2"–4" in length.

2. Decide if you'd like to leave the bark on or not. For birch logs, we often leave the bark right on for its interesting texture. Other times, we peel the bark.

3. Sand the block of wood. If the bark is removed, sand the wood smoothly on all sides. Otherwise, concentrate on the top and bottom surfaces only. Sand until you've achieved your desired smoothness.

4. Use your handsaw to create a small cavity across the center top of your log piece, just deep and wide enough to hold paper.
5. Sand again to smooth out your cut.
6. If desired, use a beeswax polish on all areas of your block to give it a bit of a smooth glow.

SOULE FAMILY FAVORITE WOODWORKING BOOKS

Carpentry for Children by Lester Walker
The Kids' Building Workshop by Craig Robertson
Woodshop for Kids by Jack McKee

ELF SOAP

KIND

(by Ezra)

TO: Lee/Molloy

FROM: Somes

Make

....

Beeswax Bobbles

Beeswax is such a wonderful medium to work with—it smells deliciously warm as it's melting in your home; it's versatile, quick, and easy to use; affordable; and a gift from nature! We like to make these little bobbles to add to our holiday gift giving. A simple string loop allows them to easily attach to a gift or bundle of baked goods and to hang as a tree ornament. If you use beeswax candles in your home, save the tiny, clean leftovers to add to this project for a bit of color!

CRAFTING NOTE

Melting solid beeswax to a liquid state is fun and smells delicious, but it can also be a bit messy. I recommend designating a wooden spoon just for beeswax and using a layer of wax paper under your work space. The beeswax, once solidified, can be peeled right off the wax paper and saved for the next time you melt!

WHAT YOU'LL NEED

Molds for the beeswax (candy molds are a perfect size; plastic or ceramic is fine)

Solid beeswax, approximately ¼ lb. for 2 molds

Double boiler, or saucepan with heatproof bowl over it

Oil for greasing molds

Wax paper or Kraft paper (for easier cleanup)

Twine or string, cut to 6" or so (optional)

2 drops of essential oil for fragrance (choose your favorite; rosemary, lavender, clary sage, and vanilla are a few that we really love for this project; optional)

WHAT TO DO

1. Begin by cooling the molds. Keep them in a cool place (the freezer or refrigerator) until the wax is ready to pour.
2. Place a layer of paper on the table surface where your molds will sit.

3. Bring a double boiler to a boil, and insert your beeswax solid. (If you need to break up the solid piece of beeswax, remember that it will be easiest when the beeswax is warmer than room temperature.) Lower the heat to a gentle simmer until the wax is completely melted and liquid. Then stir in 2 drops of the essential oil.

4. Remove the molds from the freezer and place them on top of the paper. Spray or coat the molds very lightly with a bit of oil, which will make removing the wax shapes a bit easier.

5. Pour the wax into the molds. Don't worry if it spills a bit—it will lift right off the wax paper or the side of the molds so you can add it back to the boiler.

6. Watch the wax closely. When it just begins to get cloudy, you can make a loop with your twine and insert it at the top of the mold, just beyond the surface to create a hanger.

7. Let the molds set until firm.

8. Place the molds in the freezer on a flat surface for ten minutes or so. The wax will shrink just enough to easily remove the shapes from the molds.

9. If there are bumps or rigid edges that you'd like smoothed out on your bobbles, use your fingers or a simple butter knife to do so.

Da

....

Celebrate the Solstice

All over the world at this time of year, people are celebrating. During the darkest days that the northern hemisphere sees, we adjust to the decreasing amount of light we have from day to day. Cold weather and dark days lead us to the celebratory holiday that so many of us share, despite what we may call it individually—Yule, Solstice, Christmas, Hanukah, Kwanzaa, Saint Lucia Day, and even more. The specifics may vary on how each of us celebrates, but there is much common ground to be found in our joy as well. There is a shared silence across the globe as well a sense of the magic of this season—the magic that can be defined in so many ways, one of them being the simple earthly delight of light, brightness, and new beginning. In this time, we gather together, don our homes in festive décor, light candles, decorate a tree, and feast with friends and family. When the celebrations are over, the balance is shifted to longer days, more sun, warmth, and light for all.

OUR SOLSTICE DAY

In our family, this is one of the most treasured and special celebrations of our family year. Our Solstice Day is spent out of doors as much as we can. We take a walk, or go skiing or sledding. We measure our shadows in the Solstice sun and talk about the earth and the sun and the reason for the short day. We talk about the many ways through ancient and recent history that our ancestors have celebrated the return of the light. On our day's journey out of doors, we make offerings of food and treats for the birds and woodland creatures that we know are also beginning their own seasonal adventure of winter.

As we go in and out of our home through Our Solstice Day, we prepare for a nighttime feast. We bake bread, stock the fire with plenty of wood, tidy our home, and finish up the last of our simple gifts for each other.

Just before the setting of the sun on this short Solstice Day, we go out for one last journey into the woods for a very special Yule log for the fire. Later, we'll burn this in our outside fire as the sun sets. This is our good-bye to the lunar year we are leaving and a celebration of what is to come in the next. In silence, we watch it burn and give our quiet wishes for the coming year. We light candles from this outside fire, and begin the walk inside—toward the warmth and light of our home. There, we celebrate with feasts, toasts, and gifts in celebration of each other.

SOULE FAMILY SOLSTICE BOOK BASKET

A favorite tradition in our home is to keep a special basket full of seasonal books for all to enjoy in the holiday season. This special box or basket is placed under our tree in the holiday months, and tucked away during the rest of the year. The collection grows just a bit from year to year, while the classics remain and become even more treasured with time. Here are some of our favorite holiday reads.

Jan Brett's Christmas Treasury by Jan Brett
Ollie's Ski Trip by Elsa Beskow
Owl Moon by Jane Yolen
The Return of the Light: Twelve Tales from around the World for Winter Solstice by Carolyn McVickar Edwards
The Shortest Day: Celebrating the Winter Solstice by Wendy Pfeffer
The Story of the Snow Children by Sibylle von Olfers
Take Joy! by Tasha Tudor
Winter by Gerda Muller
The Winter Solstice: The Sacred Traditions of Christmas by John Matthews

Acknowledgments

This book was a family collaboration of the truest kind. Together, the six of us explored and created in our day-to-day life. Night after night, the two of us wrote and planned side by side as the dream of creating a book together became our reality. For the way in which that happened with grace, kindness, growth, and pleasure, we are most grateful to each other.

We thank our children—Calvin, Ezra, Adelaide, and Harper—for their daily sense of adventure as we lived out this project, for their openness and patience through all of the details, and (most especially) for allowing us to share these parts of their lives beyond our family and home. We hope we have honored your stories—they are most precious to us.

Stephen, on the occasion of his first book, would like to especially thank "Mom and Dad, for your love and unwavering support and love, always. To Trina, Mike, Sarah, Randy, Greg, Carey, Shannon and Kelly—my brothers and sisters, with all my love."

From the both of us, we would like to express our gratitude to the following people:

The wonderful folks at Shambhala Publications/Trumpeter Books whose work and company we have enjoyed once again on this book journey. Special thanks to editor Jennifer Urban-Brown, cover designer Daniel Urban-Brown, interior designer Lora Zorian, and publicist Jennifer Campaniolo.

Literary agent, Linda Roghaar, who continues to guide and support in her wonderful ways.

The writers and friends who so generously contributed their own family's seasonal traditions to this book—Amy Karol, Maya Donenfeld, Heather Bruggeman, Heather Fontenot, and Langdon Cook.

Brandie Mayes, the talented Goddess of Details, for her help as pattern editor and sounding board through this project.

Jessie Fields, for so patiently photographing our growing family, and always inspiring me with what she sees from behind that lens.

Our community of friends and family, who once again blessed us with their ideas, support, childcare, and friendship during this time.

And to all the readers of SouleMama, who touch our lives and our work in oh-so-many wonderful ways every single day.

We Thank You!
Amanda Blake Soule and Stephen Soule

Contributors

Heather Bruggeman www.beautythatmoves.typepad.com
CREATOR OF THE SUMMER'S BOUNTY SALAD AND THE
FARMER'S MARKET SALAD, PAGES 119–23

Heather Bruggeman follows the mantra, "A life that is led simply
and deliberately is a life fulfilled." To that end, she is a dedicated yogi
and yoga instructor, teacher, artist, cook, entrepreneur, mother, and
wife. She balances the necessities of life with a touch of humorous
grace. Her blog, Beauty That Moves, is enjoyed by readers for its
kind honesty, shared beauty, and simple guidance through a hectic
world. Heather resides in a small New England city with her husband and daughter in a quaint bungalow where she grows raspberries and peppermint.

Langdon Cook www.fat-of-the-land.blogspot.com
CREATOR OF TEMPURA DANDIES, PAGE 101

Langdon Cook is the author of *Fat of the Land: Adventures of a 21st
Century Forager* (Skipstone, 2009). He was a senior book editor at
Amazon.com until he left the corporate world in 2004 to live in
a cabin off the grid with his family. Now a freelance writer and
blogger, Cook has written for *Gray's Sporting Journal, Outside, Fly
Fisherman, The Stranger, Seattle Metropolitan, Northwest Palate,* and
numerous other publications. He is a graduate of the University of
Washington's MFA program and a recipient of PEN Northwest's
Margery Boyden Wilderness Writing Residency. He lives in Seattle,
Washington.

Maya Donenfeld   www.mayamade.blogspot.com
CREATOR OF NATURE'S STAMPS, PAGE 187

Maya Donenfeld lives and plays in the country outside of Ithaca, New York, with her husband and two children. She enjoys working with bits from nature and transforming recycled materials into things of beauty and utility. Her work has been featured in *GreenCraft* magazine, *Country Living, Artful Blogging, Where Women Create, Sew Hip,* and more. Maya also contributed to the book *Craft Hope* (Lark Publishing). Find her on her blog, maya*made, where she shares numerous tutorials and recipes for living a simple and creative life.

Heather Fontenot   www.shivayanaturals.com
CREATOR OF MEDITATION FOR CHILDREN AND YOGA
FOR CHILDREN, PAGES 217–21

Heather Fontenot is a freelance writer, and the coeditor of the online family magazine, *Rhythm of The Home*. She has written numerous articles on yoga and meditation for children and works as a consultant helping public schools establish funded yoga programs for their classrooms. Heather writes the blog, Shivaya Naturals, where she chronicles her life as a mother, artist, and gluten-free baker. Heather resides on the Front Range of northern Colorado with her husband and two sons.

Amy Karol   www.amykarol.com
CREATOR OF VAPOR RUB AND SLIPPERY ELM THROAT
LOZENGES, PAGES 40–41

Artist, author, and mama, Amy Karol has written two sewing books—*Bend-the-Rules Sewing: The Essential Guide to a Whole New Way to Sew* and *Bend the Rules with Fabric: Fun Sewing Projects with Stencils, Stamps, Dye, Photo Transfers, Silk Screening, and More* (both Potter Craft). She has been featured in *Mothering, Country Living,* and *BUST* magazines and has contributed craft projects to more than eight books. You can find her up to no good on her craft blog, Angry Chicken, where she cooks, makes a mess with her family, and has a good time. Amy lives in Portland, Oregon, with her husband and three daughters in a house surrounded by trees.

Recommended Reading

Exploring the Natural World with Your Children

Beletsky, Les. *Bird Songs: 250 North American Birds in Song*. San Francisco: Chronicle Books, 2006.

Beskow, Elsa. *The Flowers' Festival*. Edinburgh: Floris Books, 2010.

Boring, Mel. *Birds, Nests, and Eggs*. Take-Along Guides. Minnetonka, Minn.: NorthWord Books for Young Readers, 1998.

Brown, Tom, Jr. *Tom Brown's Field Guide to Living with the Earth*. New York: Berkeley Books, 1986.

———. *The Science and Art of Tracking*. New York: Berkeley Books, 1999.

Carson, Rachel. *The Sense of Wonder*. New York: Harper and Row, 1956.

Cook, Langdon. *Fat of the Land: Adventures of a 21st Century Forager*. Seattle: Skipstone Press, 2011.

Cornell, Joseph. *Sharing Nature with Children*. 20th Anniv. ed. Nevada City, Calif.: Dawn Publications, 1998.

Davies, Jacqueline. *The Boy Who Drew Birds: A Story of James John Audubon*. Boston: Houghton Mifflin Company, 2004.

Johnson, Cait and Maura D. Shaw. *Celebrating the Great Mother: A Handbook of Earth-Honoring Activities for Parents and Children*. Rochester, Vermont: Destiny Books, 1995.

Louv, Richard. *Last Child in the Woods: Saving Our Children from Nature-Deficit Disorder*. Updated and expanded ed. Chapel Hill: Algonquin Books, 2008.

Marsh, Janet. *A Child's Book of Flowers*. London: Hutchinson Children's Books, 1993.

Murie, Olaus J. and Mark Elbroch. *Animal Tracks,* Peterson Field Guide. 3rd ed. Boston: Houghton Mifflin Company, 2005.

National Audubon Society Field Guide to North American Birds, Eastern Region. Rev. ed. New York: Knopf, 1994.

National Audubon Society Field Guide to Wildflowers, Eastern Region. Rev. ed. New York: Knopf, 2001.

National Audubon Society Field Guide to Wildflowers, Western Region. Rev. ed. New York: Knopf, 2001.

Newcomb, Lawrence. *Newcomb's Wildflower Guide.* New York: Little, Brown and Company, 1989.

Peterson, Lee Allen. *A Field Guide to Edible Wild Plants,* Peterson Field Guide. Boston: Houghton Mifflin Company, 1999.

Rezendes, Paul. *Tracking and the Art of Seeing: How to Read Animal Tracks and Sign.* 2nd ed. New York: HarperCollins, 1999.

Robbins, Chandler. *Birds of North America: A Guide to Field Identification.* Golden Field Guide. Rev. ed. New York: St. Martin's Press, 2001.

Roth, Sally. *The Backyard Bird Feeder's Bible: The A-to-Z Guide to Feeders, Seed Mixes, Projects, and Treats.* New York: Rodale, 2003.

Stokes, Donald and Lillian. *Stokes Guide to Animal Tracking and Behavior.* New York: Little, Brown and Company, 1987.

Thayer, Samuel. *The Forager's Harvest: A Guide to Identifying, Harvesting, and Preparing Edible Wild Plants.* Cleveland, New York: The Forager Press, 2006.

Uvardy, Miklos D. F. *National Audubon Society Field Guide to North American Birds, Western Region.* Rev. ed. New York: Knopf, 1994.

Ward, Jennifer. *I Love Dirt! 52 Activities to Help You and Your Kids Discover the Wonders of Nature.* Boston: Shambhala Publications, 2008.

———. *Let's Go Outside! Outdoor Activities and Projects to Get You and Your Kids Closer to Nature.* Boston: Shambhala Publications, 2009.

Young, Jon, Ellen Haas, and Evan McGown. *Coyote's Guide to Connecting with Nature.* 2nd ed. OWLink Media, 2010.

Crafts

Adrosko, Rita. *Natural Dyes and Home Dyeing.* Rev. ed. New York: Dover, 1971.

Beard, Daniel Carter. *The American Boy's Handy Book: What to Do and How to Do It.* Centennial ed. Boston: David R. Godine, 2010.

Beard, Lina. *The American Girls Handy Book: How to Amuse Yourself and Others.* Boston: David R. Godine, 1994.

Buchannan, Andrea and Miriam Peskowitz. *The Daring Book for Girls.* New York: William Morrow, 2007.

Carey, Diana and Judy Large. *Festivals Family and Food.* Edinburgh: Floris Books, 1986.

Danks, Fiona and Jo Schofield. *Nature's Playground: Activities, Crafts, and Games to Encourage Children to Get Outdoors.* Chicago: Chicago Review Press, 2007.

Dean, Jenny *Wild Color: The Complete Guide to Making and Using Natural Dyes*. Rev. ed. New York: Watson-Guptill, 2010.

Duerr, Sasha. *The Handbook of Natural Plant Dyes: Personalize Your Craft with Organic Colors from Acorns, Blueberries, Coffee, and Other Everyday Ingredients*. Portland, Oregon: Timber Press, 2011.

Iggulden, Conn and Hal. *The Dangerous Book for Boys*. New York: William Morrow, 2007.

Falick, Melanie. *Kids Knitting: Projects for Kids of All Ages*. New York: Artisan, 2003.

Lambert, Eva and Tracy Kendall. *The Complete Guide to Natural Dyeing: Fabric, Yarn, and Fiber*. Loveland, Colorado: Interweave Press, 2010.

Martin, Laura. *Nature's Art Box: From T-shirts to Twig Baskets, 65 Cool Projects for Crafty Kids to Make With Natural Materials You Can Find Anywhere*. North Adams, Mass.: Storey Publishing, 2003.

McKee, Jack. *Woodshop for Kids: 52 Woodworking Projects Kids Can Build*. Bellingham, Wash.: Hands On Books, 2005.

Robertson, Craig. *The Kids' Building Workshop: 15 Woodworking Projects for Kids and Parents to Build Together*. North Adams, Mass.: Storey Publishing, 2004.

Stoller, Debbie. *Stitch 'n Bitch: The Knitter's Handbook*. New York: Workman Publishing, 2004.

Walker, Lester. *Carpentry for Children: Simple Step-by-Step Plans for Great Do-It-Yourself Projects*. Woodstock, New York: The Overlook Press, 1985.

Wiseman, Ann Sayre. *The Best of Making Things: A Hand Book of Creative Discovery*. Reprint ed. White River Junction, Vermont: Chelsea Green, 2005.

Whole Foods, Cooking, and Gardening

Boyce, Kim. *Good to the Grain: Baking with Whole-Grain Flours*. New York: Stewart, Tabori, and Chang, 2010.

Brown, Edward Espe. *The Tassajara Bread Book*. Deluxe ed. Boston: Shambhala Publications, 2009.

Brown, Peter. *The Curious Garden*. New York: Little, Brown Books for Young Readers, 2009.

Coleman, Eliot. *Four-Season Harvest: Organic Vegetables from Your Home Garden All Year Long*. White River Junction, Vermont: Chelsea Green, 1999.

Damrosch, Barbara. *The Garden Primer*. 2nd ed. New York: Workman Publishing, 2008.

Fallon, Sally. *Nourishing Traditions: The Cookbook That Challenges Politically Correct Nutrition and Diet Dictocrats*. 2nd ed. Winona Lake, Indiana: New Trends Publishing, 1999.

Greene, Janet, Ruth Hertzberg, and Beatrice Vaughan. *Putting Food By.* 5th ed. New York: Plume, 2010.

Hirsch, David. *Moosewood Restaurant Kitchen Garden: Creative Gardening for the Adventurous Cook.* Rev. ed. Berkeley, Calif.: Ten Speed Press, 2005.

Kingry, Judy and Lauren Devine. *Ball Complete Book of Home Preserving.* Toronto: Robert Rose, 2006.

Krauss, Ruth. *The Carrot Seed.* 60th anniv. ed. New York: HarperCollins, 2004.

Lair, Cynthia. *Feeding the Whole Family: Recipes for Babies, Young Children, and Their Parents.* 3rd ed. Seattle: Sasquatch Books, 2008.

Lovejoy, Sharon. *Roots, Shoots, Buckets, and Boots: Gardening Together with Children.* New York: Workman Publishing, 1999.

Madigan, Carleen. *The Backyard Homestead.* North Adams, Mass.: Storey Publishing, 2009.

Waters, Alice. *The Art of Simple Food: Notes, Lessons, and Recipes from a Delicious Revolution.* New York: Clarkson Potter, 2007.

Natural Healing Books

Baptiste, Baron. *My Daddy Is a Pretzel: Yoga for Parents and Kids.* Cambridge, Mass.: Barefoot Books, 2004.

Falconi, Diana. *Earthly Bodies and Heavenly Hair: Natural and Healthy Personal Care for Every Body.* Woodstock, New York: Ceres Press, 1997.

Garth, Maureen. *Starbright—Meditations for Children.* New York: HarperOne, 1991.

Hopman, Ellen Evert. *Walking the World in Wonder: A Children's Herbal.* Rochester, Vermont: Healing Arts Press, 2000.

Maclean, Kerry Lee. *Peaceful Piggy Meditation.* Park Ridge, Ill.: Albert Whitman and Company, 2004.

Nghiem, Sister Thuc and Thich Nhat Hahn. *Each Breath a Smile.* Berkeley, Calif.: Plum Blossom Books, 2002.

Tierra, Lesley. *A Kid's Herb Book: For Children of All Ages.* San Francisco: Robert Reed Publishers, 2000.

Tourles, Stephanie. *Organic Body Care Recipes: 175 Homemade Herbal Formulas for Glowing Skin and a Vibrant Self.* North Adams, Mass.: Storey Publishing, 2007.

Zand, Janet, Robert Roundtree, and Rachel Walton. *Smart Medicine for a Healthier Child.* 2nd ed. New York: Avery Trade, 2003.

Winter Solstice Books

Beskow, Elsa. *Ollie's Ski Trip*. Edinburgh: Floris Books, 2001.

Brett, Jan. *Jan Brett's Christmas Treasury*. New York: Putnam Juvenile, 2001.

Edwards, Carolyn McVickar. *The Return of the Light: Twelve Tales from Around the World for Winter Solstice*. 5th anniv. ed. New York: Marlowe and Company, 2005.

Matthews, John. *The Winter Solstice: The Sacred Traditions of Christmas*. Wheaton, Ill.: Quest Books, 2003.

Muller, Gerda. *Winter*. Edinburgh: Floris Books, 1994.

Olfers, Sibylle von. *The Story of the Snow Children*. Edinburgh: Floris Books, 2005.

Pfeffer, Wendy. *The Shortest Day: Celebrating the Winter Solstice*. New York: Dutton Children's Books, 2003.

Tudor, Tasha. *Take Joy! The Tasha Tudor Christmas Book*. New York: Philomel, 1980.

Yolen, Jane. *Owl Moon*. New York: Philomel, 1987.

Resources

Seeds and Gardening Materials

Johnny's Selected Seeds
www.johnnyseeds.com

Seeds of Change
www.seedsofchange.com

FEDCO Co-op Garden Supplies
www.fedcoseeds.com

High Mowing Organic Seeds
www.highmowingseeds.com

Natural Herbal Products & Supplies

Mountain Rose Herbs
www.mountainroseherbs.com

Bulk Herb Store
www.bulkherbstore.com

Dyeing Materials & Supplies

Dharma Trading Company
www.dharmatrading.com

Sprouting Supplies

The Sprout People
www.sproutpeople.com